SONS OF THE MOVEMENT

SONS OF THE MOVEMENT
FtMs Risking Incoherence
on a Post-Queer Cultural Landscape

Jean Bobby Noble

Women's Press
Toronto

Sons of the Movement: FtMs Risking Incoherence on a Post-Queer Cultural Landscape
by Jean Bobby Noble

First published in 2006 by
Women's Press, an imprint of Canadian Scholars' Press Inc.
180 Bloor Street West, Suite 801
Toronto, Ontario
M5S 2V6

www.womenspress.ca

Canadian Scholars' Press/Women's Press gratefully acknowledges financial support for our publishing activities from the Ontario Arts Council, the Canada Council for the Arts, the Government of Canada through the Book Publishing Industry Development Program (BPIDP).

Library and Archives Canada Cataloguing in Publication

Noble, Jean Bobby

    Sons of the movement : FtMs risking incoherance on a post-queer cultural landscape / Jean Bobby Noble.

Includes bibliographical references.

ISBN 0-88961-461-X

    1. Female-to-male transsexuals--Textbooks. 2. Female-to-male transsexuals--Identity--Textbooks. 3. Transsexualism--Social aspects--Textbooks. 4. Gender identity--Social aspects--Textbooks. I. Title.

HQ77.9.N62 2006   306.76'8   C2006-901412-4

Cover design, text design, and layout: Brad Horning

06   07   08 09 10   5 4 3 2 1

Printed and bound in Canada by Marquis Book Printing Inc.

Canadä

TABLE OF CONTENTS

LIST OF ILLUSTRATIONS

ACKNOWLEDGEMENTS

AS AN ACTIVE LABOUR OF LOVE, *SONS* WAS A LONG TIME COMING. TO THE very generous manuscript readers at CSP/WP, I return the respect, courage, and faith you have lent to this project. To my colleagues, grad students, and undergraduate students in the Women's Studies department at the University of Victoria, I offer my continued good wishes and deepest thanks. My time with you in the corridor and classrooms at UVIC remains precious.

Sons would not even have seen the light of day had it not been for the exceptional vision of Dr. Althea Prince. Your presence is in each word Althea; it is my hope that they honour you.

Camille Isaacs, manager of book production at Canadian Scholars' Press/ Women's Press, has made what could have been stressful seem smooth and seamless. Thank you for seeing this through with grace.

I owe the following a debt of gratitude for providing intellectual companionship, friendship, and the queerest of context: Ummni Khan, Rinaldo Walcott, Robyn Wiegman, Susanne Luhmann, Bob Wallace, Anna Camilleri, Sarah Trimble, Eleanor MacDonald, Patricia Elliot, Laura Doan, Les Feinberg, and Proma Tagore.

Sylvain C. Boies also deserves special thanks for holding the pieces he holds.

As always, to OmiSoore: the body of this book bears witness to your fierce femme audacity, intelligence, and fire that continues to heat up my life.

INTRODUCTION

EACH OF THE CHAPTERS ARE ORGANIZED IN RELATION TO THE TERMS "trans-gender" and/or "trans-sexual," but what these terms mean is another story.[1] Even a cursory look at the social histories of the words themselves, as well as the burgeoning field of trans studies, can tell much about the value and importance of the performances, artists, and counter-discursive spaces theorized in this book. But each chapter here also marks a relation to my previous book, *Masculinities without Men?* (UBC Press 2004). That book, and its prior life as my doctoral thesis, raised, and then by necessity, both delayed and deferred the meddlesome questions that have become *Sons of the Movement*. *Masculinities* raised questions about my own relationships to masculinity, gender transitions, bodies, sexuality, and so forth, questions I refused to traffic through that physical incarnation (Ph.D. candidate) and space (institutional exercises). On the other hand, *Sons* shapes its theoretical trajectories deliberately around, on, and through the occupation of both a different time (what I'm going to call post-queer), but also a differently modulated space. These are traces of a transed FtM body, a body simultaneously inside and outside of both genders, working institutionally in a similarly housed Women's Studies department, but also trans-geographically (situated in a new city but theorizing a past in Toronto). *Sons* insists on being hailed precisely by those unanswered intertextual questions. *Masculinities*, then, echoes and resonates throughout *Sons*, quite wilfully, as its moment of origin, but also, like any moment of productive origin (something we might also mark as trauma), it tenaciously haunts as an accidental and unknowable moment of return. As I argued in *Masculinities*, the relationship between female masculinity and trans masculinity does its best work, when those resemblances function as dependent traces of each other, rather than as anxious performative deflections. So it is only fitting that, in many ways, the argument here continues to elaborate that relation. Let me write it this way: *Masculinities* is to *Sons* what a pre-transition body is to its post-transition iteration: a ghostly presence where everything is the same except for its *différance*.

What I am calling trans studies has reached a level of sophistication and self-definition that firmly establishes it as a field with its own theoretical and political location. Of course, connections to feminist and queer theory, and increasingly to transnationalism and anti-racism persist, but while these connections might share a critique of misogyny, heteronormativity, homophobia, and racism, the methodologies and goals of each field differ, often dramatically when intersectional frameworks are not deployed. Significantly, though, I am increasingly convinced that it is no longer viable for feminist readers to dismiss the projects of trans theorists and activists as acrimonious to or outside of feminist discourses. Nor is it tenable, I will argue, to view trans studies as an optional "extra" in discussions of anti-racism or studies of sex, gender, and queer theory. This book, and the work it documents and theorizes, represents an intersectional challenge to each of these fields while also simultaneously situating trans studies as and within a field of its own. But it certainly warrants repetition: I am seeking discursive and political relations, not distance.

"Trans-sexual" and "trans-gender" are essentially contested terms within and outside trans communities, and part of what is at stake in this work is the relation between established sex, gender, and sexuality labels on the one hand, and these emergent categories of new configurations of genders on the other. More than the term "queer," the prefix *trans-* itself captures what we imagine are various kinds of sex and gender crossing, and various levels of permanence to these transitions, seeming to signify everything from the medical technologies that transform sexed bodies, to cross-dressing, to passing, to a certain kind of "life plot," to being legible as one's birth sex, but with a "contradictory" gender inflection, "trans" is rapidly becoming a free-floating category, signifying its own discursive history as much as any, all, or, at times, none of the above. For example, the prefix *trans-* just as often marks a space of movement across national affiliations or identifications. Recent calls for papers, as one example, explore relations between trans-gender and trans-sexual and transnationalisms in an increasingly globalized and diasporic world order dominated by the growing terrorism of American foreign policy. I do not see queer functioning with the same connotative value in these instances. But even within the U.S., if the most recent election is any "real" indicator, the term "American" just as often marks a space of disidentification with its public image. The appearance, after the re-election of George W. Bush, of apologetic Web sites, is a curious phenomenon. The first one was set up by student James Zetland immediately following the 2004 U.S. presidential election. His Web site www.sorryeverybody.com carried the message "We're sorry. We Tried. Half of America by thousands of Americans sending out apologia to the world," which indicates, if anything, that the U.S. continues to be marked by an internal civil war, something perhaps easily described by the term "transnational." The notion of transnationalism is one lived on and through the bodies of the racialized and nationalized diasporic citizenship. Transnationalist writers such as Dionne Brand, Makeda Silvera, Rinaldo Walcott, and others clearly take up and problematize notions of belonging and citizenship in any context, not the least of which is a queer, i.e., White, queer citizenship. By emphasizing the importance of this trope, I am certainly not detracting from the importance of such work. But as I will explore more fully in Chapter 4, in this post-colonial and postmodernity era of deconstructing—sometimes literally imploding—nation-states, including queer nations, I want to ask a series of questions about the trope of *trans-* for rethinking the disembodiment of whiteness and nation as a universal signifiers.

At it most evocative, *trans-* is descriptive, marking lives lived across, against, or despite already engendered, sexed, national, and even racialized bodies. Often collapsed into "trans-gender," that umbrella term that references almost all of the above practices from one degree to another, the term "trans-sexual," for instance, is thought to mark the use of medical technologies to correct the disjunction between the body and a self that seems at odds with that body. But at its most provocative, *trans-* and the space it references refuses the medical and psychological categorical imperatives through which it has always been forced to confess. As Foucault has taught us, confession is always already an overdetermined discursive practice, choreographed by regimes of power (1982). In the case of trans-folks, confession and the legitimacies it accords have often demanded congruency between so-called changed desire and object choice; between chosen gender and sexual conservatism; and, most pernicious, between sex and gender themselves.

But what is also at stake is a politics of self-representation within and often opposed to these violently policed dualistic options. Central to this polemic, then, has to be something of a paradox for trans-folks seeking images of themselves/ourselves: how does one represent oneself when one's self has unrepresentable (within current and often conservative categories) forms, practices, and discourses? Hence, the importance of trans-art and, I hope, *Sons of the Movement*, both have created a space in which to represent the unthinkable overdetermined by binaristic gender schemas but also beyond the celebration of contradiction itself. What I call for here is a political deployment of contradiction and incoherence against the intersectional hegemonies of the White supremacist, sex/gender system.

An almost century-long series of lessons of feminist gender theory have been significant. Trans-work builds upon well-established deconstructions and complications of the relationship between sex and gender. If the term

3

"gender" refers to the process whereby concrete individual subjects are constituted as subjects of a pre-existing social category, then, as Gayle Rubin suggests, the sex/gender system, or those sets of arrangements that perform this task, function best by cloaking their operations and implying that their effects are those of nature instead. Recent scholarship in the fields of queer studies, gender studies, and trans studies all expose and trouble the technologies and cultural infrastructures that construct gender as an unchanging biological essence.

That crisis is significant because when you really investigate centres and margins, we learn that the terrain is never quite as simple as it seems. Early feminist theory all but collapsed the causal link between sex and gender, but curiously, queer theorists such as Judith Butler and Eve K. Sedgwick cautioned against such ruptures. It is true that Sedgwick, in particular, built upon Rubin's call for analytical distance between these terms, but Sedgwick also held in reserve the necessity of fully exploring the epistemological links between them. That is, when Sedgwick writes in Axiom 2 that "the study of sexuality is not coextensive with the study of gender," she certainly solidifies the significant paradigm shift launched by Rubin. But Sedgwick concludes that axiom with the following: "But we can't know in advance how they will be different" (1990: 27). We can analytically assume then, that in what I have called elsewhere this No Man's Land of queer and trans-genders, that while they—sexuality, sex, and gender—are different, we also need to assume that "different" does not necessarily mean unrelated as hegemonic and historical categories. Butler too draws this out not only in *Bodies That Matter*, but also in her new work, *Undoing Gender*, suggesting that "to understand gender as a historical category, however, is to accept that gender, understood as one way of culturally configuring a body, is open to a continual remaking, and that "anatomy" and "sex" are not without cultural framing" (Butler 2004: 10).[2] Even as we pull these terms apart, an equally tenacious and conservative set of rhetorics and practices at the heart of the sex/gender system continues to fold one back into the other. Sometimes that folding occurs quite incidentally inside our movements just as often as outside.

The subjects inhabiting the No Man's Land—a stretch of contestatory and discursively productive ground that no man nor woman can venture into and remain a coherently ontological and natural subject—are marked by relations between sexuality and gender, although one of the assumptions I hope this book will correct is that we no longer need to think in terms of that relation. On the contrary, we still know far too little about its various internal, albeit non-essentialist, operations. Clearly, as both Judith Halberstam and I suggest, one of the other subjects, but nowhere near the only subject, repeatedly misread but persistently entrenched within No Man's Land is female masculinity. Female masculinity references a range of subject positions—drag king, butch, female-to-male (FtM) trans men, both operative and non-operative, trans-gendered men, stone butches—simultaneously constituted by irreducible contradictions between (de)constructions of "bodies" misread in a certain way as "female" and yet masculine.

But that subject is not alone in No Man's Land. While it is also true that no one of these practices is reducible to the other as exemplary of female masculinity, it is also true, within the logics of this deconstruction, that the category of female masculinity, as I argue in *Masculinities without Men?* (2004), works best when it marks spaces defined away from the conventionally defined female body as well as the male. That is, one of the arguments I make in that earlier work, an argument that I want to develop in *Sons of the Movement*, is that our conceptual work in rethinking the feminist sex wars, and our work on the butch-femme renaissance of the late 1980s, which anticipates the emergence of FtM masculinity, all suggest that many of our tools continue to assume, and by implication, renormalize a kind of coherence of the essentialized body.

For instance, much of that work began to reclaim the figures of butch-femme sexual cultures of the 1950s and, despite opposition, shed light on what were at that time long-forgotten practices of hetero-gendered butch-femme erotic systems. Sally Munt, Lynda Hart, Judith Halberstam, and others acknowledge that the phrase "butch-femme" references homosexual (differences in sexual orientation), but in terms that are hetero-gendered (differences in gender identifications) and that centre erotic practices that emerged in post-World War Two urban working-class lesbian communities in the United States. These practices were driven underground after a harsh condemnation by lesbian-feminism in the 1970s, but reappeared in the early 1980s after the acrimonious sex wars; this condemnation, of course, was and remains akin to the same vitriolic hysteria meted out toward trans-sexual women. Butch-femme communities share with trans identities a need to battle narrowly defined gender polemics, or so it seemed.

But more recently, debates around butch-femme have overlapped with those around trans-gender and trans-sexual (not at all the same thing) discourses necessitating a similar shift in language from "butch," referencing particular forms of lesbian masculinity, to "female masculinity," or particular types of gender expression that bring together both ends of that phrase while, at other times, refusing the distinction altogether (Halberstam 1998a). At stake in many of these debates are the ways in which female masculinity has erroneously become coterminous with ontological "lesbianism" (not all female masculinities are lesbian; not all lesbians are masculine; not all lesbians are female). When pressure is placed on the fault line between masculinities, the limitations of heteronormative (read: binaristic) configurations of gender, embodiment, and identities are exposed in the fissure. All too frequently, lesbian configurations of identity that strive toward stability and certainty also have assumed a kind of concordance between body shape and gender category, a concordance that has reproduced the limitations and sometimes the violence of a naturalized biological essentialism. They have also assumed (at times dictated) a coherence between the categories "butch" and "woman." But if this narrative holds, then what lies at the heart of the contradiction mapped by the phrase "female masculinity" remains a subject where bodies and subjectivities must remain, by definition, in contradistinction. What then of one subject, the female-to-male trans-sexual man, for example, who moves toward eliminating that distinction? Such subjectivities remind us that not every subject of female masculinity necessarily wants to mark himself as such. Is it possible then that this newly configured category ("female masculinity") remains singularly lesbian and not transed? It seems that the sex wars are not over at all.

One of the places where they have resurfaced and where sex, sexuality, and gender fold back into each other has to be the British Columbia case *Kimberly Nixon vs. Vancouver Rape Relief and Women's Shelter*. Kimberly Nixon is a male-to-female (MtF) transsexual woman who has been living as a woman for 19 years. In 1995 Nixon signed on for the Rape Relief training program at the Vancouver Rape Relief and Women's Shelter, but was eventually ejected from the process when, after a series of questions, she was told that Rape Relief did not allow "gay men" in the training sessions. When Nixon made it clear that she was, in fact, not a gay man but a post-operative male-to-female transsexual, Nixon was told she was not welcome to continue the training. The case went before a British Columbia Human Rights Tribunal where Nixon won her charge of discrimination, but VRRWS is appealing the decision on the grounds that a person who grew up as a male lacks the personal history and life experience to sensitively counsel women who have been raped or abused by men. What's particularly interesting about the case is the work that is being done across feminist organizations attempting to define and stabilize the definition of a "woman." In their appeal, VRRWS claims, by implication, that the experience of victimization and sexual abuse is the cornerstone of the definition of woman. Even if the courts themselves cannot adequately answer the question "What is a woman?", some women's organizations have attempted to weld together victimization and femininity, tyranny and manhood. Such essentializing assertions, whether trans-phobic in intention or "only" in consequence, attempt to fix not only the limits of gender but also the intelligibility of what counts as the experiences of the appropriately gendered body. That supposedly "female" body is knowable through a teleological narrative overdetermined as a history of victimization. Gender, then, is reduced to experiences that, according to VRRWS, have nothing to do with the body and yet everything to do with the maturation experiences of that body all at the same time. (Do all women really have the same experiences and experience the same trajectory from birth to death?) And both the body and gender are reducible to what is visible and discernible.

Admittedly, we can dismiss the trans-phobic resistance to Kimberly Nixon's presence in VRRWS as (conservative) feminist politics gone wrong. But what about the case of the person *Sons of the Movement* will claim as a FtM trans hero, David Reimer? To date, very few trans-cultural workers and academics have taken up Reimer's case, despite his suicide in 2003. Important caveats by Halberstam and Hale about claims made on the dead notwithstanding (1998), David's case is worth pausing over. Like many other trans-folks I've had conversations with since hearing of David's suicide, I was struck by the degree to which his movement through genders, despite his birth into a male body, uncannily resembles many of the stories of FtMs. David's story seems to come into the public realm in and around 1967, when he and his twin brother were circumcised at the age of seven months. As the story goes, David's is botched and as a remedy, David's family agrees to a somewhat unusual, controversial, and seemingly far-fetched treatment. That remedy—sexual reassignment surgery and treatment—launches the career of Dr. John Money, who uses David's case to build an argument against essentialist causation in favour of social construction. The treatment fails and at age 18, David begins a process of reassignment into a masculine identity, one that he claims in John Colapinto's *As Nature Made Him* (2000) as well as in other interviews was his natural identity all along. So, the trajectory of David's identity has been from M to F, then to F to M again, where we understand that these multiple "M's" and "F's" are not themselves necessarily even equal to each other. As evidence of this, "David" was not even his actual birth name; it was the name he chose after transitioning back into what he characterized as his birth identity. David's birth name was Bruce; David's first reassigned name was Brenda; his twin brother, who committed suicide several years before David, was named Brian.

The degree to which Dr. Money medicalized trans- and intersexed identities is evident in David's story as it was told to Colapinto. These seem to be always already mediated narratives, perhaps even and especially for David, but the narrative he and David produce are telling for the stakes of the medicalized management of appropriately sexed and gender bodies. The lives of David, Bruce, and Brian were significant and while I certainly am not claiming a definitive interpretation, I remain convinced that each is worth including within the frameworks of post-queer incoherence. It is significant that David has left behind a legacy of interviews as well as his book with John Colapinto and even though we may not have agreed on the "cause" of gender identities, David's story continues to haunt any narrative of the medicalized (mis-)management of gender identities. What becomes very clear in David's story is the degree to which his gender identity, regardless of where and how it came to be, was somewhat established by the time his MtF reassignment took place. After his FtM reassignment, David recounts memories of himself as a boy as well as a strong male self-image. But what is also clear is the degree to which David and his brother were both forced to endure abuse at the hands of Dr. Money in the name of treatment and corrective therapy. For instance, Colapinto reports memories from both Brian and David about the use of pornography in teaching children about the supposed difference between male and female genitals (Colapinto 2000: 86), but even more disturbing were memories of visual self-inspection (inspecting each other's genitals) and simulated sex, which was:

> First introduced when the twins were six years old. Money, [Brian] says, would make Brenda assume a position on all fours on his office sofa and make Brian come up behind her on his knees and place his crotch against her buttocks. Variations on the therapy included Brenda lying on her back with her legs spread and Brian lying on top of her. On at least one occasion, Brian, says, Dr. Money took a Polaroid photography of them while they were engaged in this part of the therapy. (Colapinto 2000: 87)

Again, regardless of how one accounts for the production of gender identity (the nature vs. nurture debate), these accounts of sexual abuse passing as "therapy"—that is, sexual abuse in the name of compulsory heterosexuality and forced and coercive engendering—should be enough to fold these issues directly into both a feminist agenda and issues of social justice. To date, there is nothing but silence about these types of abuses of children (of any gender) in the name of heteronormative corrective management.[3] If we presume, as we can, that Brian and David were not isolated cases, then how is it possible that these are anything other than feminist issues? Moreover, David's chosen identity and his experiences as they are detailed in *As Nature Made Him* are those of an FtM, at least for part of his life. So, at the same time, then, how could David (and even his brother Brian) not be a trans hero(es)? And why are we, as trans activists and academics, not championing his trans story?

And given the poverty of our sexual and gender categories, where might we place David: Queer? Heterosexual? Homosexual? None seems to fit particularly well, which tells us that our categories are already out of date. Hence the need for the term "post-queer" in my subtitle. Part of the work I want *Sons of the Movement* to accomplish—beyond carrying stories like David's to their necessary audiences—is to challenge the existing and available categories we have for classifying both our lives and our social movements. I will return to a discussion of the impoverishment of our categories later in Chapter 1, where I argue that for me as an FtM who has had a long life as a lesbian that I do not renounce, the oversimplistic and invested categories of "man," "lesbian," "butch," and even "FtM" are not flexible enough to name my experiences. If I call myself, as I do, a "guy who is half lesbian," where does that fit? I want to begin documenting in this book the realities and lived experiences of those of us who might be verging on incoherent, post-queer landscapes. As I will posit here, it seems that "queer" is beginning to become an unusable term; it has the potential to be centripetal or stabilizing the space it marks, or centrifugal, that is, destabilizing the spaces it flags (as in to pervert, torsion, make strange). While I am convinced, for instance, by Ann Cvetkovich's argument that each of these markers—"queer" as much as "lesbian"—are insufficient as monolithic spaces, relations, categories, etc., it seems to me it's time to call for another—dare I say a post-queer—refinement of our languagings (Cvetkovich 2003).

Nowhere is this refinement more evident than in the smallest but most resonant traces that mark the "I" we live through: gendered pronouns. When "gender" no longer references "sex," then the pronouns "he" and "she" can no longer reference a discernibly gendered body. In this book, I will use pronouns strategically, including my own, to reference what I identify as post-queer rearticulations of counter-discursive subjectivities and practices. If subjects are in dialogue with discourse and speak it as often as they are spoken by it, then the processes of "self-articulation" are themselves meta-discursive. That is, they are about those discourses as much as they are of and in opposition to those discourses, hence the importance of trans-cultural work in mapping these discourses both on the same map with, but certainly on a different grid, from those mapped by feminism, queer theory, and gay, lesbian, and bisexual studies. Butler names the stakes: "That feminism has always countered violence against women, sexual and nonsexual, ought to serve as a basis for alliance with these other movements, since phobic violence against bodies is what joins anti-homophobic, antiracist, feminist, trans, and intersex activism" (2004: 9). That said, within intersectional methodologies and frameworks not all violences against bodies are equal, nor are they extraneous to these movements. To be White, as I will argue in Chapter 4, means to be situated relative to systemic violences whether intentionally enacted or not. Again, to quote Butler: "Sometimes norms function both ways at once, and sometimes they function one way for a given group, and another way for another group" (2004: 8). I recognize that for me, "becoming male" is a lifelong process. I also recognize at the same time that White masculinity has been, not to overstate the case, an agent of near-genocide, death, violence, terror, and destruction. *Sons of the Movement* is, I hope, situated in both of these truisms and calls for a radical politic of deconstructing White masculinity as much as many of us need to step into these admittedly post-queer categories all at the same time.

Sons of the Movement also theorizes the post-queer spaces in one specific location—Toronto—as significant to the culturally specific situatedness of trans-ness as it emerges within the city as a construct itself. The completion of this book occurred as I left Toronto to begin my work at the University of Victoria. While I have been happy to leave behind many aspects of a large urban centre—pollution, noise, traffic, endless line-ups, etc.—I find, on the other hand, that it is precisely the diversity offered by such a city that enables livable, sustainable political, social, and aesthetic practices. I have not lost my ambivalence for Toronto since leaving it, but even as I write, I know that *Sons of the Movement* is part memoir, part emotional archive and testament, but like all good memoirs, it is also a social and critical history of present politicized communities and artistic practices in No Man's Land. Mine is one snapshot of a life well lived in one geographical location, but it remains singular and, I am certain, an invested reading as it is always already autobiographical.

That said, the questions raised by these post-queer skirmishes in No Man's Land are the questions shared by both trans studies and contemporary scholarship in gender and sexuality studies: What is masculinity? Femininity? What is gender? And how is gender related to bodies? This book suggests that answers to these questions are to be found in cultural artifacts: texts, performances, and/or images that explore engendered and trans subjects. Those artifacts are the stuff of, quite literally, life-changing cultural work and the important questions raised and documented by *Sons of the Movement*.

Chapter 1 develops many of the conversations of the introduction, although it begins to elaborate on the differences in these identities/identifications in a more autobiographical way. I tell the most recent part of my own story here through the two primary men in my childhood: my father, who was a closeted gay man, and my grandfather, who came to Canada as one of the Barnardo children. Barnardo ran a series of orphanages throughout England at the turn of the 20th century as a strategy to deal with the increasing number of street children. The Barnardo homes and affiliates struck a deal with the Canadian government to ship these "little immigrants," children between the ages of 12–18, to Canada to work in the kitchens and fields of Canadian farms. The violent, exploitative, and abusive experiences of these children are well documented; my grandfather was one of the "Barnardo boys" and I trace a genealogy of my own class and gender through these two very different working-class men in an attempt to elaborate on trans-rearticulations of manhood in No Man's Land.

Chapters 2 and 3 explore theoretical questions around female, male, and trans-sexual masculinity within the larger context of masculinity in popular culture and White masculinity in several Hollywood films: *Gangs of New York*, *Fight Club*, and *8 Mile*. Here I consider the resurgence of the boy as a gender identity in car television commercials, boy bands, recent Hollywood films, and postmodern theory. Chapter 3 in particular reads for that boi/boy in queer popular culture what Kathleen Martindale called un/popular culture. The objects I choose to look at here are not all produced in Toronto: for instance, *Girl King* is a brilliant film made by a West Coast femme film-maker, Ileana Pietrobruno (2003). But if anything links these performances of boy culture together, it must be my own personal culture of consumption, which was Toronto, a far different culture of reading practices than those in Victoria. This chapter will read the relationship between masculinity, race (including whiteness), class, and sexuality by analyzing the performances of several local drag kings who are resident members of Toronto's No Man's Land—Susan Justin ("Stu") and Deb Pearce ("Man Murray" and "Dirk Diggler")—as well as other Toronto drag king troupes: KingSize Kings, New Cocks on the Block, and the first ever group of kings in Toronto, The Greater Toronto Drag King Society. Drag king performances resignify masculinity through various postmodernist strategies, including parody and ironic reiterations of song lyrics. Man Murray, on the other hand, takes aim at the whiteness and the gender contradictions of Canadian singer Anne Murray. Layering recognizable performances of female masculinity onto a "failed" performance of heteronormative femininity, Man queers that which has signified queerly for decades: Canada's own butch national icon. Where *Man* interrogates queer genders, *New Cocks on the Block* stage wilful incoherence as a strategy of resistance.

Sons of the Movement argues for an intersectional, post-queer politic of incoherence as a strategy of resistance. Where the two tropes can seem quite similar, they do, it seems to me, mark different social spaces with different connotations. As I will argue later, queer had as part of its original deployment a willful separation from gay and lesbian. Even though the term "queer" is relatively recent as a signifier of anti-normative rearticulations, it does have a complex, acrimonious, and dialogical gay and lesbian history that is worth detailing. Clearly, it is evocative of strangeness, but it is also parasitic in its historical deployments. It is almost common knowledge by now that its negative history is a shaming insult that allows for its tenacity as a tool to resist those practices too. Butler details the logic of this reversal as a Nietzschian "sign-chain," where the history of a custom or word can be a continuous chain of ever-new meanings and interpretations (1993: 224). In queer contexts as in queer theory, the term is not at all meant to be synonymous with "gay," "lesbian," "bisexual," or "transgender." As de Lauretis indicated in the infamous *Differences* issue where she launched a deployment of queer:

> the term "Queer Theory" was arrived at in the effort to avoid all of these
> fine distinctions in our discursive protocols, not to adhere to any one of the
> given terms, not to assume their ideological liabilities, but instead to both
> transgress and transcend them—or at the very least problematize them.
> (1991: v)

Yet, the term still adheres to its connotative currency as a noun, a thing, and as a space decidedly gay. In *Queer as Folk*, for instance, the supposed harbinger of all things queer, recall Brian's face-to-face debate with Michael in a faux-Toronto gay bar about marriage. Michael, who does end up marrying Ben while in Canada, argues for the right to step into gay marriage while Brian argues vehemently against it, claiming "we're queers; we don't get married." But while queer is supposed to mean more than gayandlesbian, all too often, as in *Queer as Folk*, it also marks the default space of "gay male" culture. For instance, Ruth Goldman suggests that many lesbian feminists have resisted the term because of the degree to which it erases gender and, by doing so, risks reducing an analysis of gender-based oppression to one of sexuality instead (Goldman 1996: 171). Curiously, though, not all feminist theorists resist the term and this is where the waters become productively murky. Gloria Anzaldúa, for example, embraced the political anti-racist space marked by "queer" in a way decidedly unmarked by "lesbian." The latter, she argues, marks distinct Anglo-European roots and associations while the former appears as a positioning in many cultures even if the word does not. Still, though, Anzaldúa herself was cautious about any word that functions as a monolithic imperative: "Queer is used as a false unifying umbrella which all 'queers' of all races, ethnicities and classes are shoved under. At times we need this umbrella to solidify our ranks against outsiders. But even when we seek shelter under it we must not forget that it homogenizes, erase our differences" (Anzaldúa 1991: 251). But third wave theorist Astrid Henry marks a potential new deployment of the term "queer." In her controversial *Not My Mother's Sister: Generational Conflict and Third-Wave Feminism*, Henry argues that the use of the term "queer" in feminist contexts marks a shift from second to third wave feminism. In a chapter provocatively called "Neither My Mother Nor My Lover," she writes: "While 'queer' is not always deployed to mark a generational changing of the guard in the guard in the manner intended by the third wave, many self-described queer writers have used the term precisely in order to mark a generational shift that identifies them as distinct from the lesbians and gay men who came of age in the 1970s and 1980s" (Henry 2004: 116).

These resignifications—sign-chains—are what Mikhail Bakhtin identified as the dialogisms of language in lived contexts. One of the central premises of Bakhtin's work is the parallel between the construction of texts and the construction of the self. Both centripetal (stabilizing uses of language and meaning) and centrifugal (uses of language that destabilize meaning, allowing for resignifications) forces intersect through a term like "queer," which is not the product of a closed system but of social acts or "active participant[s]" that respond to and anticipate other utterances (Bakhtin 1981: 233). Because Bakhtin's concern rests with language as living speech in its concrete totality (what Bakhtin means by "discourse"), he suggests that the meaning of any linguistic sign is diachronic and relational, involving different speakers and their use of words within sentences. Where de Lauretis might have wanted to defer discursive protocols and ideological liabilities, the lesson from Bakhtin suggests that if language is inseparable from its specific socio-historical context, then those protocols and liabilities tenaciously persist: "Language acquires life and historically evolves [...] in concrete verbal communication, and not in the abstract linguistic system of language forms" (Bakhtin and Medvedev 1978: 129). The results of these context-determined utterances are meaning-making processes dependent upon contexts. Language as discourse is productive, and relations of language evoke present, past, and possible future contexts as well. Thus, it follows that the constitutive nature of a word like "queer" itself embodies a multiplicity of meanings and traces of its past usages.

> Utterances are not indifferent to one another, and are not self-sufficient; they are aware of and mutually reflect one another. Each utterance is filled with echoes and reverberations of other utterances to which it is related by the communality of the sphere of communication [...] Each utterance refutes, affirms, supplements, and relies on other [...] and somehow takes them into account. (Bakhtin 1986: 91)

If language is the space of confrontation between differently oriented accents or what de Lauretis described as protocols, then by speaking and hence rearticulating and "languaging," subjects transform both the social context in which speech occurs and themselves as well. These transformations are what constitute language as dialogic. Stuart Hall rereads Bakhtin to posit that subjects are formed and, by implication, reformed "new" *vis-à-vis* discourses and utterances. Conversely, since subjects are "languaged" by discourse, so they must use and reconfigure those same discourses to, as Hall puts it, "construct some narrative, however impoverished and impure, to connect the past and the present: where they came from with where they are" and indeed where they are bound (Hall 1996: 143). In turning these texts, discourses, and dialogic languaging processes upside-down, rendering them incoherent, or at least refusing their cohering, subjects remake themselves, becoming and exceeding what they are, finding a meaning that fits, however temporarily, and only, as Bakhtin reminds us, until its next moment of refraction.

> When a member of a speaking collective comes upon a word, his own thought finds the word already inhabited [...] there is no access to one's own personal "ultimate" word [...] every thought, feeling, experience must be refracted through the medium of someone else's discourse, someone else's style, someone else's manner [...] almost no word is without its intense sideward glance at someone else's. (Bakhtin 1984: 202–203)

"Queer" is a word, a set of ideological liabilities, a set of protocols even, increasingly its own box marked by so many " intense sideward glance(s)," both toward gayandlesbian but also occluding their shared blind spots of trans-gender and trans-sexual—that is, it is becoming a term that marks everything and, by implication, absolutely nothing at all. That is, it seems to be that "queer" is beginning to become unusable; it has the potential to be centripetal or stabilizing the space it marks (as in the show, *Queer as Folk*, marking queerness and masculinity as coterminous) or centrifugal—that is, destabilizing the spaces it flags (as in to pervert, torsion, make strange).

I have also been influenced here also by Calvin Thomas's work on queering heterosexuality. Thomas argues that such resistances to the regimes of the normal are not exclusive to gay, lesbian, or bisexual practices. Such queerings can be part of anti-heteronormative practices among heterosexual practices as well. But cannot a practice of resistance, of incoherence, also be a strategy for resisting regimes of White supremacy as well? It is harder to place queer in this context, that is, of challenging the coherence that is to accrue between whiteness and masculinity. To render something incoherent means three things simultaneously: first, it means a lack of organization or a failure of organization so as to make that thing difficult to comprehend; second, it also means failing to cohere as a mass or entity; third, in my OED, one final meaning suggests "having the same frequency but not the same phase." The reading of a body as gendered male and racialized White involves presenting signifiers within an economy where the signifiers accumulate toward the appearance of a coherently gendered and racialized body. Becoming a transsexual man, for me, however, means occupying the permanent space of not just becoming; that is, it is a permanent place of modulation of what came before by what comes after, never fully accomplishing either as an essentialist stable "reality" but also of permanent incoherence if the subject is to matter at all. But it also means rendering bodies and subject positions as incoherent as possible to refuse to let power work through bodies the way it needs to.

Chapter 4 explores the link I referenced earlier between trans-gender, transsexual, and transnational through my own body as a White trans man. Here, I theorize my own relationship to/as whiteness through a transed body, arguing that for White trans men in particular, an active anti-racist practice is imperative. That we transition into a masculine identity is not enough; we must also self-consciously and wilfully embody an anti-racist, anti-White supremacist politic at the same time. The first step toward that practice, which is really a practice of being a race traitor, is to understand that our White bodies are articulated in a larger grid of power over which we have little control. To create strategic interventions, then, means stepping into whiteness with the goal of fully, intentionally, and with an understanding of the consequences of our actions, create as much race trouble as gender.

For the work in Chapter 5 on queer fem(me)inity, I apologize to femmes everywhere. It is problematic indeed to include queer fem(me)inity in a book with such a gendered title (i.e., "sons"). But these performances I detail in Chapter 5 are a necessary and gendered parallel to the border wars surrounding the "sons" of the feminist movements. Chapter 5 is a cultural analysis and historiography of femme performance artists and femme cultural production in Toronto. Reading queer/trans performances of femininity in popular culture through a character like Sally on the television show "3rd Rock from the Sun," this chapter explores the space that is finally daring to speak its own name: queer femme. Writer and performance artist Anna Camilleri articulates femme subjectivity through her own work in *Boys Like Her*, but also through a new collection of writing, *Brazen Femme* (2002). Camilleri has also curated a number of very important lesbian/queer cabarets—Strange Sisters held at Buddies in Bad Times Theatre—which have showcased femme poets, performance artists including Pretty, Porky, and Pissed Off, dance troupes and so on, all of whom queer both femininity and the presumed masculine demeanour of lesbian subcultures. This queering, I argue, needs to be reconfigured as an emerging trans-gendering of subjects relegated to the historical margins of lesbian genealogies. These are the "strange sisters" of the sons I document and are a necessary set of players in the post-queer cultural landscape for which I call.

The final chapter of this book explores the photographic record of FtM bodies and the workings of one film, Ileana Pietrobruno's *Girl King*, to argue that these are trans- bodies by choice. These are bodies that cross the essentialized gender divide to create gender trouble. All too often, folks tend to make judgments about the political efficacy of transsexuality and trans-bodies without ever having really seen that body. I explore in this chapter visual documents that detail these bodies. *Sons of the Movement* deploys a metaphor of trenching through No Man's Land, then, where to trench upon means "to encroach upon [...] or to verge upon [the] borders" between queers and trans-folks; between FtM but gay trans-sexual men and gay men; between heterosexual women and heterogendered women and trans-sexual women; between MtFs and FtMs; between non-operative FtM trans men and butch/lesbians and the trans- sensualists who seek out both. If any word, as Bakhtin suggests, is both already inhabited and a social event, the expression and product of listeners and speakers, then the resignification of words and the performances of those resignifying practices are precisely what is at stake in both the code-crossing and riots of meanings that are fought on and over the words "man," "woman," "whore," "lesbian," "butch," "male to female," "female to male trans-sexual," and so on. At its most conservative and violent, the sex/gender system cannot make provisions for the willful production of incoherence inherent in the nature of language, or what this book will name as a dialogic, or double-, indeed, multi-voiced, post-queer collision of utterances and discourses articulating bodies—indeed, bodies of articulation—at the end of the 20th and early into the 21st century. Some of those incoherencies are recorded here.

NOTES

1. In *Masculinities without Men?* I spelled "trans-gender" and "trans-sexual" with a hyphen and explained that:

    > I write *trans-sexual* and *trans-gender* for several reasons … the suffix *trans* often is used to suggest that its subjects, those referenced by either the *sexual* or *gender* which follows the suffix, somehow 'transcend' gender by 'exploding' the binary gender system. These subjects do transcend the discourses of the sex/gender system that ground all meanings of gender in the appropriately sexed body. But to say that these subjects 'transcend' gender seems to suggest that they do not find themselves articulated by gender. They most certainly do embody and perform gender difference. But the body which houses that performance is a *transnatural* body produced with the help of science, endocrinology, surgeries, etc. (Doan: 152). Thus, I write *trans-sexual* and *trans-gender* with hyphens to defamiliarize the way that these terms manipulate and produce gender difference by deploying what I will call an alibi of gender essence, an alibi provided by the sexologists and clinical psychiatry that authorizes interventions if the correct narrative is present. Again, these discourses do not transcend gender but are instead productive of subjectivities that are rewritten/re-articulated by those same subjects. I hyphenate to foreground these productive but troubling relations between bodies, subjectivity, discourse, temporalities and languages that, albeit perhaps only contingently, eventually produce something resembling (trans-)gendered subjects. (Noble 2004: 159)

    This is worth repeating here. I'll explore this further in Chapter 1.

2. Even as I quote from Butler's new book, it remains important to note that the criticisms of Butler's work by trans activists still stand (see, for instance, Namaste 2005 and Prosser 1988). While Butler is careful in this new work to acknowledge and theorize a plethora of gender queers as well as the differences between them, she uses the very problematic term "new gender politics" to characterize their

importance. What's noteworthy is that these social movements and theories are nowhere near "new" in 2004 and many have been living, breathing, challenging, and protesting against the gender hegemonies of the sex/gender system and queer and feminist theory for at least four decades, if not longer, since the very first sexual reassignment surgeries were performed in the 1960s. These occlusions, the very ones conditioned by Butler's performative "new," are precisely the stuff of frustration and acrimony, begging the question, "When is new?" Answer: Perhaps when it is noteworthy by the big names of theory? I too will reference these trans-genders, but for what I hope are different purposes.

3. There are notable exceptions. Anne Fausto-Sterling, Suzanne Kessler, and Susan McKenna detail and challenge, along with activist groups, like the extremely important Intersexed Society of North America, the abuses of both intersexed and children diagnosed with gender identity disorder by both homophobic and heteronormative medical practitioners.

Chapter 1

SONS OF THE (FEMINIST) MOVEMENT: TRANNY FAGS, LESBIAN MEN, AND OTHER POST-QUEER PARADOXES

THE TITLE OF THIS CHAPTER—INDEED, OF THE ENTIRE BOOK— references Julia Creet's 1991 essay "Daughters of the Movement: The Psychodynamics of Lesbian S/M Fantasy," which theorized the dynamics of the sex war that raged throughout the 1980s. These debates, conflicts, and extremely acrimonious battles circulating around questions of feminist sexual practices began, so our mythologies tell us, around several very early events: the publication of *Heresies #12: The Sex Issue* (1981) and the 1982 Barnard College conference "The Scholar and the Feminist IX" (Vance 1983). In fact, Patrick Califia has suggested that the opening missives of the sex wars occurred as early as 1977–1979 in San Francisco (Califia 1982). The sex wars seemed to end shortly after the publication of Judith Butler's paradigm shifting treatise *Gender Trouble*, a text that, again, as our mythologies have it, co-parented the spawn of the sex wars: *Queer Theory* (1990). Creet's paper also made important interventions in these debates, arguing that one of the most consistent tropes in lesbian s/m writing was the motif of the good feminist mother and the "bad" irreverent daughter (Creet 1991). I borrow my title from Creet's work to secure these arguments in the histories of feminist acrimony. This chapter argues that it is now time to deal with the most recent border war within feminism/women's studies: that of trans-sexuality.[1] But I want to locate both my argument as well as its content within feminist histories of acrimony. It might seem strange—deliberately evoking a history of tension within the feminist movement—but I think such tensions and, more often than not, our *inability* to resolve them rather than our erasure of the conflict constitute the critical possibilities of feminist scholarship rather than its failure.

In her book, *Am I That Name? Feminism and the Category of "Women,"* Denise Riley makes a similar assertion (1998). Arguing that feminism needs to refuse to locate itself in categorical and essentialist foundations, Riley suggests instead that feminism might entertain the possibility of contingency, indeterminacy, and instability as a willful epistemology and politic. Given that these passionate fictions of gender, sexuality, embodiment, class, race, nation, and ethnicity are all historically specific and enmeshed with the lived histories of other concepts like, for instance, the social, the subject, constructions of power, the mind, the soul, the body, capitalism, and economics, etc., then, Riley asks, why does feminism attempt to secure its politics to a fixed and ahistorical essence of gender? Leaving behind the "why" question, Riley and others argue that any strategy that attempts to ensure victory through fixity rather than flexibility cannot win in the long run. If the sex/gender system and its rhetorics of biological determinism work by stabilizing gender essences, then why attempt to build a politic on that same supposed self-evidence of the body? Such corporeal self-evidence is precisely the stakes of the border skirmish under discussion in this book.

I also evoke the concept of history here for another reason. I want to articulate this work within my own personal history as a White, formerly working-class, trans-sexual man *inside* the feminist movement. Like many trans-sexuals—and despite a panic to the contrary—I come to this current border war with a long feminist history: I came out as a working-class lesbian in my last year of high school, 1978. I found the word "lesbian" in the very important feminist book *Lesbian Woman* by Del Martin and Phyllis Lyon (1972), and after asking myself "Am I that name?", I answered "yes." After a brief stay in late 1980s Toronto, I made my way west to Edmonton, Alberta, where I spent almost a decade working inside the lesbian feminist movement. My pre-academic resumé details much of this work: I did almost four years with the Edmonton Rape Crisis Centre; I was part of the lesbian caucus of the Alberta Status of Women Action Committee; I organized and took part in far too many Take Back the Night marches. I was one of a very small group of people to organize and march in Edmonton's first Gay Pride Parade (about 1987 there was seven of us; we walked for a block and then ran for our lives). I have spray-painted the sides of more buildings than I care to remember; I took the very first "Women and Literature" course at the University of Alberta with Professor Shirley Newman; my feminist poster archive includes an original 1979 Toronto IWD poster, but also a huge and very battered *YES* poster, which was part of the 1976 American ERA equal rights amendment campaign. I started and sustained through two Edmonton winters a sex-worker advocacy group called the Alliance for the Safety of Prostitutes, a group that met during the coldest winter nights in the only gay bar in Edmonton. I was "the" out lesbian for many television and radio interviews and published many activist articles, pamphlets, and tracts in a variety of feminist and lesbian feminist newspapers and magazines. I have helped build many parts of our activist movement long before I entered university and claim this history quite proudly.

I do not find my home in the word "lesbian" any longer (although that's often my dating pool), but I want to be very clear that I am not here as a trans-sexual man knocking at the door of the feminist movement asking to be let in. I have been *in*, *of*, and indeed, have been *the* feminist movement and in my work on masculinity, and in my burgeoning identity as a trans-sexual man, I continue to wear that banner with a great sense of history and with a great deal of pride, if not frustration some days. I belabour this very personal introduction because I want to make it clear here that instead of imagining that female-to-male trans-sexual men are inside the Trojan horse when we come into the feminist movement, we need to rethink our movements to understand that *trans men* are actually inside the belly of the beast when we *leave* feminist spaces. We are, like many other men, sons of the movement and feminism has much to gain by claiming its masculine progeny.[2]

That there are triangulated border wars between women's studies, lesbian butches, and female-to-male trans-sexual men (FtMs) is by now almost cliché. This relation is flagged by the paradox and/or contradiction in the statement: "I am a lesbian man." This, by the way, is not autobiographical; it is borrowed from one of the subjects of Aaron Devor's book length study *FTM* (1997) where, among other things, conventions of grammar, logic, and intelligibility fully break down under the weight of such paradoxes. Devor's strategy of using mixed pronouns to describe the same subjects and of not developing an analysis of his subjects as men has led to some very strange grammatical and discursive constructions like, for instance, "when Johnny was a little girl" or "I am a lesbian man." However, beyond these epistemological limitations of Devor's work, the categorical taxonomies and definitional border wars that condition intelligibility remain, I argue here, undertheorized.[3] Those border wars within feminism and women's studies over the subjects of what I am calling No Man's Land—female masculinity, trans-sexual masculinity, and masculinity's studies—are, I will argue, absolutely vital, not dangerous, to the future of feminism.

Such a belief—that thinking masculinity (*trans* or otherwise) in the context of feminism is its undoing—is the grammar of continued feminist scholarship like, for instance, Tania Modleski's book, *Feminism without Women: Culture and Criticism in a "Postfeminist" Age* (1991). Confusing feminist deconstruction with anti-feminist "post-feminism," Modleski rightly queries the stakes of a deconstructive feminism, but wrongly draws conclusions that are, at the very least, trans-phobic in their oversights. Modleski's book is curious. On the one hand, she interrogates the ideologies of texts that proclaim or assume the advent of post-feminism, but draws inevitable conclusions when she argues, on the other, that these are texts that are instead "engaged in negating the critiques and undermining the goals of feminism—in effect, delivering us back into a prefeminist world" (Modleski 1991:3). The strategically confused temporalities of *post-* and *pre-* notwithstanding, Modleski's work is a clear example of the kind of feminism Eleanor MacDonald critiques in "Critical Identities: Rethinking Feminism through Transgender Politics" (1998).[4] Throughout her readings of texts as varied as *Three Men and a Baby*, the phenomenon of Pee-wee Herman, as well as male masochism, Modleski never once reads female masculinity, trans-sexual or trans-gender politics, or performances like drag kinging for their productive feminist rearticulations of gender. What she accomplishes with her occlusions is the reconsolidation of a gender system that is bound by biological essentialism.

Modleski's project is an example of feminist scholarship that, to quote from MacDonald:

> [O]ften maintain[s] gender systems, albeit "alternative" ones, designed to stand in direct opposition to those of dominant society. [...] One sees [in] them [...] the continued assignment of femininity and masculinity to specific behaviors. (MacDonald 1998: 7)

In fact, the word "transgender" appears only once—in the last paragraph of the book—to reference the failure of queer politics and theory, as well as feminist masculinity studies to "break free of restrictive gender roles" (Modleski: 163). Work such as Modleski's holds out much deconstructive promise, but fails to supersede its own limited essentialist framework. The result is the complete erasure of the productive possibilities for feminism of a politic located within No Man's Land and a reconsolidation of a categorically conservative identity politic.

But these reconsolidations are not limited to feminist theory. Queer theorist Judith Halberstam and trans theorist C. Jacob Hale document similar border skirmishes in "Transgender Butch: Butch/FTM Border Wars and the Masculine Continuum," their essay in "The Transgender Issue" of *GLQ: A Journal of Lesbian and Gay Studies* (4, no. 2 [1998]: 287–310), only they examine these border wars as they emerge between trans-sexual/trans-gender politics and queer theory. Attempting to rearticulate an argument from an earlier controversial essay, Halberstam, in particular, queries the space between lesbian masculinity and trans-sexual men. That earlier essay, "F2M: The Making of Female Masculinity," generated a great deal of debate when Halberstam argued that within postmodern economies of gender, all genders are "fictions of a body talking its own shape ... for some an outfit can be changed; for others skin must be resewn. There are no transsexuals" (Halberstam 1994: 210–212). In the *GLQ* essay, Halberstam addresses the controversy generated by the earlier essay by suggesting that part of the stakes of both essays was the stabilization of the terms "transsexual," "transgender," and "butch" as unique and distinct identities, each separate from the other. Instead, Halberstam (1994: 288) writes: "One of the issues I want to take up here is what model of masculinity is at stake in the debates ... and what, if anything separates butch masculinity from transsexual masculinities," suggesting instead that what has been at stake in the border wars are the terms of gendered embodiment itself. Halberstam gestures to the strategic deconstructive experiences of trans-sexual masculinity, although, as I will argue later, she resorts back to categorical determinism when coining the phrase "female masculinity."

Clearly, what interests me about these debates is less the veracity or authenticity of these conversations (presuming such things are even possible or valued) but rather the way that these terms flag shared feminist histories, or histories of the ideas about gender and sexuality. That is, these movements—feminism, gay, lesbian, bisexual movements, the pro-feminist men's movement, and trans movements—each remind us that becoming any gender is a socially constructed process that is ongoing, contingent, non-foundational, and self-producing. That is, articulating one's self as a subject (engendered, racialized, sexed, nationed, classed, etc.) is the process through which we learn to identify our "I" relative to bodies, power grids, as well as culturally available categories like pronouns, and then attempt to become that configuration (echoing Denise Riley's question: "is my 'I' that name"?). Bound within this process are, of course, two axioms that are coterminous with those of feminism: first, not all "selves" are commensurate with and reducible to the bodies, categories, pronouns, and, indeed, bodies intelligible in the sex/gender system; and, second, not all incongruities are equal and although we cannot always know in advance *how* they will be different, we certainly do need to anticipate and correct for the ideological work these differences are doing within our social justice movements (Sedgwick 1990: 27).

These incongruities among the subjects flagged by the phrase "female masculinity" are radically de-emphasized in Judith Halberstam's extremely important book *Female Masculinity* (1998). Besides being the source of my book's title, *Masculinities without Men?* (2003), it is, after *Boots of Leather, Slippers of Gold*, the first book-length study of subjects heretofore neglected in academic inquiry.[5] *Female Masculinity* makes several important interventions in sexuality and gender studies. First, after coining the phrase "female masculinity," which works through juxtaposition—in other words, through categorical indeterminacy—Halberstam produces and then deconstructs the subjects who are now visible through that oxymoron. Halberstam herself notes the misrecognition that has collapsed the very significant differences between subjects hailed by the phrase "female masculinity"—butch masculinity, trans-sexual masculinity, trans-gendered subjects, drag kings, and so on—she argues, as remedy, that while these subjectivities might look similar, each have different representational and discursive histories. Where some of the work theorizing these subjects challenges a binary or two-genders system by positing a third gender, Halberstam's work instead gives us multiple engenderings. That is, her work is most potent when she suggests that instead of conceptualizing female masculinity and lesbianism as coterminous and thus as a singular figure between masculinity and femininity, our analytical findings are richer when female masculinity itself is understood as multiple, contradictory, and inherently plural.

But another important goal of Halberstam's work is to distinguish female masculinity as distinct from male masculinity or, as she says in an oft-quoted expression, "conceptualizing masculinity without men" (1998a: 2). In the end, she wants to make masculinity safe for women and girls, even heterosexual women, so that with more gender freedom, perhaps even men will be able to recreate masculinity using her model of female masculinity. A number of critics have read the phrase "masculinities without men" to suggest that it means without relation to men. For instance, in his review for the *Journal of Men's Studies*, Daryl B. Hill comments that "the assertion that [female] masculinity is 'masculinity without men' is problematic" (2002: 237). What Hill seems to be identifying here is how Halberstam's work, like my own, is predicated upon a rupture or distinction between "masculinity" and "men." If the term "men" is successful as both an ideology and as a signifier, then the referent it imagines itself marking is the male body, complete with penis as supposedly self-evident referent. If, however, the term "masculinity" accomplishes its work, then "men" no longer references a self-evident penis. What it references instead is that same sex/gender system that feminism has identified and critiqued, only now we see it operating on a new site: masculinity. "Men" collapses the distinction between signifier and referent. "Masculinity" not only reasserts it but suggests that the possession of a conventionally defined penis has nothing to do with securing manhood. Masculinity is a free-floating signifier, detached from that referent. So when we posit that sometimes masculinity has nothing to do with men, we are not necessarily arguing literally that female masculinity is not related to male masculinity.

Instead, the argument is that masculinity now has nothing to do with the male body as it has been conventionally defined. Both trans and female masculinity are each non-derivative forms of manhood where that subject is no longer secured or privileged by a referent.

That said, the irony of Halberstam's accomplishment is that it is achieved through a series of problematic disavowals. The major difference between Halberstam's work and mine is that my own work cannot and will not sustain the disavowals at the heart of Halberstam's argument. First, and perhaps less immediately significant but still glaringly problematic, is the question of the taxonomizing impulse that organizes Halberstam's inquiry. That this categorical imperative is confusing has already been noted in a number of reviews that agree that *Female Masculinity* suffers from an excessively schematic taxonomy, where the solution to the problem of categorical thinking is to come up with still more categories. Why Halberstam chooses this particular tactic is puzzling. But what seems clear is the effect of this impulse: I argue that *FM* is a text primarily concerned with lesbian masculinity while I hope to articulate a post-identity politic and post-queer, anti-heteronormative—that is, counter-cultural—trans-masculinity. What Halberstam's categorical imperative accomplishes is that it produces an odd alignment of sex and gender that should be most powerful when it refuses categorization altogether. What I want to offer through FtM trans-sexual men is a feminist refusal of essentialist categorical schemas. Post-queer—that is, trans-gendered and/or trans-sexual—but not gay and/or lesbian subjects are, by definition, newly configured masculine subjects and bodies that deconstruct in the flesh the terms of hegemonic gendered embodiment and do so in proximity to masculinity.

These relationships among men of different genders within similar class, racial, sexual orientations, etc., are the deconstructive *stuff,* as it were, of trans-sexual masculinity. Halberstam suggests and declares a performative *indifference* toward male masculinity that she hopes will pass as an affirmation of female masculinity. "Such affirmations," Halberstam (1998a: 9) writes of female masculinity, "begin not by subverting masculine power or taking up a position against masculine power but by turning a blind eye to conventional masculinities and refusing to engage [...] power may inhere within different forms of refusal: 'Well, I do not care.'" On the contrary, I make no such disavowals. In fact, I am interested in taking up a subject position precisely in and as a male subject, although one schooled, as I have alluded in the beginning, as one of the sons of lesbian-feminism. The subjects I am theorizing—not lesbian men but FtM tranny men and boys—are subjects who find power not by feigning indifference but by cultivating proximity, identification, and similarity with other subjects of masculinity. Can we entertain the possibility that sometimes, some "lesbians" actually *do* want to become men? The argument that female masculinity does not notice, or is not influenced by, or does not reciprocate nor return the gaze to male masculinity cannot be supported. Each instance of masculinity is unquestioningly informed, influenced, mentored, and otherwise learns to become itself from other men in their class or race. FtM tranny guys—either as trans-gendered or trans-sexual—not only have to directly "engage" the men around them, they must also, to turn a clichéd phrase, embrace the boy within themselves in order to move closer to becoming him. Halberstam's "I do not care" might work as a rhetorical disavowal but, like all disavowals, as there are moments where subjects cannot know what it is they both already know and are always already constituted by, it certainly begs the question of psychic proximity to and identification with masculinity, not distance.

That said, proximity and repetition with a critical and strategic distance is crucial for those of us who want to become political men. I want to suggest that masculinity simultaneously needs to be reconfigured as a deconstructive fiction as well. Such deconstructions must be predicated upon two things: an intersectional model of thinking identity and a permanent rupture or distinction between "masculinity" and "men" but also upon a strategic necessity of that rupture. Given the first premise of intersectional theories of social construction, each subject of any identification is also articulated in and through different classes, races, ethnicities, abilities, sexualities, and bodies at the same time. These relationships among trans men of different genders within similar class, racial, sexual orientations, etc., are not only the stuff, as it were, of trans-sexual masculinity but they remain the measure of its critical potential as well. Let me come at this from a very real fear and criticism within the context of feminism about these transitions into masculinity. One of the most frequent critiques I hear about FtMs is the assertion that by "crossing over this divide"—that is, by transitioning and therefore becoming men—FtM trans-sexual men are now living a kind of privilege not accorded to lesbians or biological women and so, as a result, are somehow betraying their feminist sisters. I have been troubled by this critique—that of crossing over—but it's been only quite recently that I have been able to discern what is at stake in its metaphors. While I recognize that the presence of masculinity in feminism has been complex, the topography of this metaphor recognizes only one singular battlefield (to continue using a troubling metaphor). That is, part of what this criticism does is to reduce the complex distributional matrix of power to the site of gender only. If there is only one side that is good and one side that is bad, then we are back to models of thinking that are singular and non-intersectional. Similarly, this model of thinking also paints masculinity with one simple brushstroke as "bad" and antithetical to feminism. If our model of feminist critical practice privileges a singular mono-linguistic identity only (gender), then so be it; FtM trans-sexual men have betrayed the cause. But, within the intersectional models of identity—where we understand power is distributed through a matrix of identities simultaneously—then this criticism of FtMs cannot hold.

What this criticism actually reveals when it seeks and thinks it finds privilege accruing to gender is, first, its own inability to think intersectionally and, second, its complete erasure of whiteness as a mark of power. Let me phrase this differently: When we think we're seeing FtM trans-sexual male privilege, I suggest that what we're actually seeing is whiteness modifying masculinity to give it power. If, for instance, trans-gendered "women" of colour transition into FtM trans-sexual masculinity, we'd be quite remiss to suggest that this FtM is transitioning into a privileged gender position in our culture. There's absolutely no way that we can say, in good conscience, that a trans-sexual man of colour has more power than a White, born-female, heterosexual feminist, can we? So if I have more power as a White trans-sexual man than I had as a trans-gendered and extremely masculine lesbian, is it not my whiteness that is articulating power through my gender? Especially when we consider that FtM trans-sexual surgeries are not producing passable bodies; they are producing intersexual, hybrid bodies that are outside of our gender taxonomies and queer lexicons. Whiteness, as so many have told us, works invisibly to modify and articulate identity, but White supremacy also aggressively de-privileges particular groups of men in our culture while distributing power quite happily to others. It seems to me that these criticisms, then, of FtM trans-sexual men are bound within non-intersectional models of thinking identity within White supremacy, which either tell us more about the anxieties of whiteness or tell us a great deal about the limitations of our theoretical paradigms.

Having said that, it is important to acknowledge here that some groups of men do have more privilege than others. To be sure, White, middle- to upper-class men absolutely have more power; heterosexual more than queer; bio men more than trans men. It is not at all my intention to suggest otherwise, but can we not also suggest that embodiments of masculinity are privileged differently in proximity to hegemonic imperatives of the sex/gender system? That is to say, one of the other things that worries me about this categorical dismissal of FtM trans-sexual men is the way in which it also tells us something about how we are thinking about the transitional process itself. For FtMs more than MtFs, the transitional process is one fraught with categorical indeterminacy. FtMs almost never fully become men; they stay in the place of transit even if some strike a hegemonic bargain with masculinity that is similar to that of whiteness. That is, to be a trans man means to accept and to allow others to accept, as James Baldwin suggested about whiteness, a hegemonic fiction, albeit a powerful one. "White people are not white," suggested Baldwin, "part of the price of the white ticket is to delude themselves into believing that they are" (Baldwin 1985: xiv). That is, they accept the hegemonic bargain that traffics in a fantasy of primary, pre-colonial, universal, and racially unmarked whiteness. Baldwin is in conversation with historical thinkers like Sojourner Truth and W.E.B. Du Bois, but also anticipating contemporary theorists like bell hooks, Ruth Frankenberg, Chandra Mohanty, Gloria Anzaldúa, and many more women who have argued that there is no such thing as pure categorical whiteness. The existence of the now newly configured non-intersectional White race produces the unconscious (at best) willingness of those assigned to it to place their racial interests above class or any other interests they hold. Whiteness, in other words, is bound by and is, in effect, secured by its imperative of universal, categorical singularity (that is, non-intersectionality). Entrance into this fictionality of whiteness is purchased through an ideological belief in naturalized whiteness. I will return to a discussion of the politics of whiteness in Chapter 4.

Kessler and McKenna suggest something similar in their early work, *Gender: An Ethnomethodological Approach* (1978). They argue that the perception of a fixed gender role is just that—a perception interactionally and pragmatically coded by the external signifiers of gender. "Gender attribution of a complex, interactive process," they write, "involving the person making the attribution and the person she/he is making the attribution about" (Kessler and McKenna 1978: 6). The "reading" of a body as legibly gendered, they suggest, involves presenting gender signifiers within an economy where the signifiers accrue toward the appearance of a coherently gendered body. Becoming a trans-sexual man, however, means occupying the permanent space of incoherent becoming (to transit: n. & v., going, conveying, being conveyed, across or over or through, passage route ...); that is, it is a permanent place of modulation of what came before by what comes after, never fully accomplishing or cohering either as an essentialist "reality." For me, as an example, this permanent state of becoming means also failing to become the type of man unknowingly privileged in our culture. I have lived for almost 30 some years as a lesbian feminist first and this training ground has made me one of the best, although strategically failed heterosexual men you're likely to find. One of the key things for me in this "transition" is a refusal of what we've identified in feminism as the hegemonic imperatives of adult manhood. Along with John Stoltenberg, the "Michaels" Kimmel and Kaufman, Stuart Hall, and so many other very political pro-feminist men, I have refused and continue to refuse the privileges of becoming a man in the hegemonic ways this category is constructed. Instead, I have opted to occupy the pre-man space of boy/boi, which I argue elsewhere is a productive failure. I have done this by, among other things, maintaining the discursive space of F on my identification papers, by living and working in lesbian and queer circles, by working against White supremacy, capitalism, and so on. These juxtapositions between how I present, my categorical refusal to be fully "manned" either in language or in body (Bob or Robert vs. my boi name of Bobby), but also my refusal to step into the discursive space of M to match my gender presentation, signal the critical, political, but also discursive space of tranny masculinity for me outside of the clinical and medicalized treatment of trans-sexual bodies. This often puts me, in daily practice, into some very interesting positions where my presentation trumps the F, and where I politically refuse the mechanisms of manhood—taking up space, for instance, in male ways, or jockeying for position with other men for the alpha male position. Instead, I ally myself with anti-racist practice or encourage other men, as an educator, to remain boys instead of becoming manly men, but, most importantly, I strategically refuse power (not responsibility) if women and/or men of colour and/or gay men are present to assume that power instead. These allow me a daily deconstructive practice that aggressively refuses the hegemonic fantasy of "manhood." Part of what I am trying to say is that there are many different ways of being masculine; there are many different subject positions available for men, some of which have more power than others. If this is true, then there are many different subject positions for FtMs to transition into (masculinity as modulated by power). As a tranny-man, then, it is my constant practice to refuse that hegemonic bargain by refusing to become that kind of man. What I seek as a trans man is radical modulation and categorical indeterminacy rather than categorical privilege. The trans space of masculinity needs to be reconfigured as a concept of negative space, which, like any other concept of negative space, is only as effective as the things on either side of it. As a critical practice, then, we might embody a disidentified space of woman, yes, but the space of disidentification only means in so far as it informs the simultaneous refusal to become a hegemonic man at the same time. It's the relation that matters here, hence the need to think paradox: I am a guy who is half lesbian.

My own work on and through these border wars of feminism, FtM masculinities, and male masculinities does not just map these proximities; I advocate for the social, psychic, and political necessity of these relationships. Post-queer relationships among men are often at different angles to each other politically, even though we are not likely to see the masculine version of the television show "Will and Grace" (could we even imagine, let's say, "Bubba and Butch" or "Spike and Mike"), the space between men and butches or between men and FtMs—male masculinity and female masculinity can be a productive space. Female to male trans-sexual bodies are bodies that not only matter—and need to matter a great deal to feminism—but, as I have argued elsewhere, these are bodies that defy matter. Both female and trans masculinities have much to offer a gender politic: in addition to the necessary reconceptualizations and deconstructions of masculinity, these subjects, especially trans masculinity, offer us a new way to defamiliarize heterosexuality. To be sure, politicized transed men can embody a feminist anti-normative heterosexuality and more often than not, queer both it and masculinity (if by queer we mean pervert, challenge, de-form). That, it seems to me, is a project that feminism might want to embrace to stay vital in the 21st century.

NOTES

1. The Graduate Programme in Women's Studies at York University held a very important day-long symposium called "Transgender/Transsexual: Theorizing, Organizing, Cultural Production" where a version of this paper was presented on November 29, 2002. Thanks are due to Linda Brisken.

2. Much of this is not new at all. See Alice Jardine and Paul Smith, eds., *Men in Feminism* (New York: Methuen, 1987), Steven P. Schacht and Doris W. Ewing, eds., *Feminism and Men* (New York, New York University Press, 1998), as well as an important new collection, Judith Kegan Gardiner, ed., *Masculinity Studies and Feminist Theory* (New York: Columbia University Press, 2002). But what my book seeks to do is to claim a space for masculinity in women's studies without this having to mean the end of feminism. What it can mean is an even more potent gender politic and deconstructive program for the 21st century.

3. The space surrounding trans-sexuality and feminism has been theorized in the work of feminist scholarship already. See essays by both Eleanor MacDonald and Patricia Elliott, to whom this book owes acknowledgements.

4. Modleski's invocation of a simultaneous post- and pre-feminism suggests, rhetorically and self-servingly, that feminism hasn't occurred at all yet and supports her assertion that a progressive, theoretically sophisticated and politically effective

feminism needs to return to its own limited and historically bound moment of origins, something third wave feminism is attempting to and needs to transcend. This temporality is reiterated in the final sentence of the book: "The postfeminist play with gender in which differences are elided can easily lead us back into our 'pregendered' past where there was only the universal subject—man" (Modleski 1991: 163).

5. I was reminded of *Boots of Leather, Slippers of Gold* (by Elizabeth Lapovsky and Madeline Davis) in conversation with Elise Chenier, whom I thank.

Chapter 2

"ZOOM, ZOOM, ZOOM": EMERGENT BOYZ, BOIS, BOYS IN POPULAR CULTURE[1]

THE POLITICAL EFFICACY OF TRANS-SEXUAL MASCULINITY IS IN DIRECT proportion to the feminist efficacy of masculinity in general, which, as a number of critics have argued, is now undergoing a crisis. That crisis and the many ways that masculinity has been codified recently into the field of masculinity studies or men's studies as an integral part of gender studies is riddled with many productive and politically surprising contradictions. I want to explore some of those contradictions here by looking at recent constructions of masculinity in popular culture. We can claim, for instance, quite legitimately, that men have no history. We also have at least 30 if not more years of feminism telling us that all history is men's history. Isn't every history book a history of men? Have we not also learned from feminist scholars that it has actually been women who have had, until recently, no history? How is it possible for us to reconcile these two contradictory points? The first step toward making this argument requires an acknowledgment that despite the many books on or about men that fill up even the smallest bookstore shelf, such works do not necessarily explore the self-conscious experience of knowingly being a man, and of how the discourses and knowledges of manhood structure the lives of men, the organizations and institutions they have created, and the daily events in which they participate. Men still have no self-conscious history of themselves as subjects of masculinity.

What would it take then to write *of men* as men? What does that mean? Obviously, writing as men requires a critical consciousness of masculinity as a gender. But it also requires a consciousness of the historicity of masculinity, of its differences from other gendered subjects, and, as I will suggest soon, its differences from itself. One of the first premises of masculinity has to be an inversion of what Simone de Beauvoir (1953) first said about "Woman" in *The Second Sex*, that is, that woman is made, not born. Similarly, the first premise of any study of masculinity must also be that men are similarly made, not born. But, more accurately, we might also say and this is premise number two: Masculinity, like any gender, is as much made as unmade and thus must be reimagined over and over again. What does that mean? It means for a man to speak about his gender in a critical, self-conscious manner already means that somehow he has failed to live up to the patriarchal ideal and imperative that he not *think* and *know* masculinity but that he just *be the man*, which means to be the universal subject. Consequently, his masculinity is already in trouble. If our culture has built a series of coterminous relationships between power, physicality, and masculinity whereby either of those terms can stand in as synonyms for the other, and where women are defined in terms of their sex and men as the bearers of a body-transparent personhood, then those same mechanisms bind men in a series of inarticulate contradictions while simultaneously articulating masculinity as a universal subject.

To put this slightly differently, why is it that there is no heterosexual male counter-discourse that would compare to those of gay, feminist, and anti-racist liberation movements? What are the languages of heterosexual masculinity? Why is there no comparable, deconstructive, political counter-discourse for straight White men that can do the work of self-consciously separating masculinity from the persistent and contradictory grip of traditional masculine ideals and imperatives? Masculinity, as the realization of a set of ideals and imperatives about a presumption of a particular type of body, a script, and power, emerges in the 20th century as a set of symptoms continuously and unrelentingly anxious about failure (Thomas 1996). Heteronormative masculinity, which is profoundly undone by its own fear of failure and thus proving one's manhood (meaning not being feminine and being male enough), has become one of the defining features of being a man. Part of what I will be reading for in this and the next chapter are the ways that the imperative to be a man is uttered within a logic, as Butler (1990) indicates about heterosexuality, that secures its impossibility. One of the effects of this impossibility is a proliferation of masculine subject positions, each produced and constituted through contradiction.

The first step toward discerning masculinity and seeing it no longer as the universal subject but rather as a particular realization of ideals and imperatives about masculinity will require making gender visible to men. This certainly has been one of the functions of drag king cultures. And by gender I mean the sets of cultural meanings and technologies that, in the case of masculinity, have allowed power, an imaginary construction of the male body, and masculinity to all function as synonyms for each other. I want to argue through the performances of masculinity under discussion here, beyond being merely constructed, they invariably unfold as a series of authorized imperatives or scripts about what masculinity should be by simultaneously flagging what it should not be. The effect of these imperatives is not necessarily to authorize one type of masculinity over another but to naturalize those performances as if they were imperatives from nature itself, not culture and discourse.

Several critical theorists take these imperatives apart, albeit in different ways, with different epistemological methodologies and in different forms. Jackson Katz's documentary, *Tough Guise*; John Stoltenberg's collection of semi-autobiographical essays entitled *Refusing to Be a Man*; and William Pollack's psychological study called *Real Boys* each work in entirely different ways to similar outcomes: the documentation of the representational, political, and psychological stakes of this crisis. *Tough Guise* is a lovely and very teachable documentary on the relationship between masculinity, toughness, and popular culture. As narrator in *Tough Guise*, Jackson Katz explores the changing and invested representations of masculinity to argue that in order to intervene in this crisis, we first need to change our definitions of what Katz identifies as "normal" constructions of manhood to see what's coded into them. What he discovers is very similar to Bhabha's answer—that is, the notion of masculinity as guise, a posture, is the culture of manhood. He argues that the guise is a survival posture so intense that "just being one of the guise" is no longer a description but a violent imperative: be tough or be unmanly. It is an unspoken set of codes among men that are reinforced by images of popular culture, which disseminates these constructions with tremendous and deadly hegemonic force.

Pollack also identifies this in his study, *Real Boys: Rescuing Our Sons from the Myths of Boyhood* (1998). Echoing Katz's notion of the guise, Pollack argues that this guise functions for boys as a set of injunctions, a boy code. What is this boy code? Pollack's answer is that perhaps the most traumatizing and dangerous injunction thrust on boys and men is the literal straightjacket that prohibits boys from feeling emotions to avoid being perceived as feminine. The primary objective of the boy code is to assure the perception of heterosexual, hard, impenetrable manhood through performances or guises that distinguish him as different from "females" and "homosexuals," but also that distinguish him as the tough guy. Pollack's work on this code through case studies and interviews demonstrates the how's and when's and why's of what Katz identifies as the end result, the adoption of the prosthetic guise.

In *Refusing to Be a Man*, Stoltenberg begins to identify these politics of masculinity very early in his career, but also very early in the second wave of feminism. He is writing in the early 1970s and his antidote to masculinity is to refuse the guise, refuse to become a man, that tough guy. Stoltenberg (1988: 3) challenges the impossibility of growing up to be a man and becoming a feminist, asking, "What would happen if [men] told the deepest truth about why we are men who mean to be part of the feminist revolution—why we can't not be part of it." It has, I think, taken a long time before Stoltenberg receives answers to his political questions. But nevertheless, his refusal, as a political refusal, begins to expose and challenge the guise, the boy code, or what he himself described as "what goes on in men's minds and bodies and lives in order to maintain their belief that they are 'men'" (Stoltenberg 1988: 4). At the very least, all three, as a small sample of theorists and critics across disciplines, suggest to us that something is going on with masculinity.

To be sure, certain coded performances of masculinity as guise are socially and politically sanctioned and authorized over others (heterosexual over gay, for instance), but part of what we need to notice are how these differently authorized performances of masculinity compete for authenticity, what Butler (1991: 24) calls "reality effects." Given that one of the goals of this book is to render invisible genders more visible, then thinking of masculinity in these ways is bound by a curious contradiction, for straight men, articulating themselves as men, begin to speak and/or think of their identities as an activity that is overdetermined. To be self-conscious about oneself as a man means to be already suspect as a man. That is, developing a conscious discourse of manhood is a potential sign that a man has failed to become a man in the hegemonic ways—that is, without consciousness. Toward a presentation of an answer to this dilemma, what we can suggest instead is that instead of being an effect of nature, masculinity is not a thing; rather, masculinity is a set of signs and signifiers, discourses, media images, and scripts that overdetermine what we think we recognize as masculinity. Similarly, masculinity and the male body are not reducible to each other, but each is articulated through the other. The result is that, in a sense, it might be possible to argue that all men are male impersonators who "embody" and "perform" those scripts (Simpson 1994). Rethinking masculinity as male impersonation outs a kind of performance anxiety—that is, most men are never entirely sure that they are performing it correctly, especially since figuring out what those scripts are is part of being a man. The words "man" and "manly" have become freely floating signifiers with few (if any) referents in an economy where that which has always wished to be seen as monolithic, normal, and natural has become fragmented, particular, and denaturalized.

As a consequence, then, there are particular questions I am interesting in asking of the performances of masculinity I study here. First, what is it that masculinity cannot know about itself but which might be visible in the rituals of language use or imagery or performance? That is, what is being shown to us that the subjects of these discourses might not be able to know about themselves as men? And second, how are the tensions, desires, fears, ambivalences, and contradictions of being a man in this culture worked out on stage, in performance, in social movements, or through the symbolic relations between men, both fathers and sons, but also among men or boys outside of relationships with women? And by Father/father here I mean both metaphorical or symbolic cultural Fathers, not only actual or literal fathers. Is the quest of masculinity to be in the "right relation" to the father in order to become a man?

In order to flesh this crisis out in a bit more detail, I want to look at one very successful film about masculinity: *Fight Club*. In order to read this film for its complexities, it is vital to understand the degree to which masculinity is increasingly commodified by late 20th-century capitalism and hegemony. For years, feminism has taken aim at capitalist beauty myths, a set of ideas and practices that construct the arbitrary category of beauty for women as an unreachable ideal based on, among other things, standards of White femininity, thinness, and so on. I would argue that the discourses, practices, and ideals of the beauty industry have also now taken masculinity into its grip, as it were. We have the development of new psychological disorders for men (for instance, *The Adonis Complex*), which I think is far greater evidence of the beauty myth's dependence on capitalism more than anything else. This new disorder—muscle dysmorphia—has been documented by Pope, Phillips, and Olivardia (2002), and marks a gendered condition, similar to anorexia for women, in which men are unable to see themselves in a mirror without seeing their worst fears, which for men is an unfit body. The remedy is an excessive number of hours working out at the gym. What's more telling is that capitalism and the beauty industry have recently discovered something that Naomi Wolf and Susan Faludi both detail for women: that commodity capitalism seems to be providing what it imagines to be the remedy to this crisis, which it may well be, at least in part, creating.

Having said this, the beauty industry has responded to this crisis by attempting to reconsolidate masculinity through tropes of muscularity. That is, if part of this crisis is productive and is evidence now of an increasingly counter-hegemonic view of masculinity as socially constructed as less hyper-masculine, then we can argue that we are seeing a kind of backlash against this notion from ideas of male beauty. Some statistics might help this picture: If over 25 million men do some kind of body work; if about 20 percent of all liposuctions are done on male bodies; if American men spend about $9.5 billion annually to improve their physical appearance; $3.3 billion on grooming products like fragrances, deodorants, and hair-colouring treatments; $4.27 billion on gym/health club memberships and exercise equipment; $1.36 billion on hair transplants, wigs, and hair restoration; and $507 million on cosmetic surgery, then surely these numbers tell us two things: First, that male beauty is not an issue that should be so easily ignored and, second, masculinity is increasingly becoming as stereotyped, idealized, and commodified in our culture through pop culture (Dotson 1999). The question we want to ask here is this: If men's bodies are now increasingly in the forefront of cultural, hegemonic, but also capitalist scrutiny, then what's at stake in such regulations?

In a deeply thoughtful essay, "'See Me, Touch Me, Feel Me'" (Im)Proving the Bodily Sense of Masculinity," Marc Ouellete brings that question and its answers directly in line with feminist practice (2005). Ouellete tracks changes in what he calls the technologies of embodiment for the male body (echoing Foucault), to argue that these technologies are transforming the terms of embodiment to produce what he calls a "New Man." Those more conventional practices (surface improvement-like changes made through clothing and hairstyling), but also new procedures like those detailed above—surgical hair implants, plastic surgery, chemical body modification, and so forth—have not only generated this "new man" vis-à-vis a new image of the male body, but they've also reconfigured masculinity as the object of the gaze. Where John Berger argued in his book *Ways of Seeing*, that "men watch, while women watch themselves be watched," what Ouellette is discovering is that increasingly, men are also watching themselves be watched. If Berger was right, that one of the effects of these looking relations for women is a split and fractured self-image constantly haunted by an idealized image, then, we might be able to argue that capitalist hegemonic beauty and culture industries have found another market. Masculinity may well be similarly fractured as men are similarly haunted by an over-idealized image of the powerful male body. This new phallic power is now more purchasable than ever. Ironically enough, for this new man, like the trans man (about whom I'll say more in later chapters), the male body itself is not natural but is instead a kind of prosthetic, something built, created, and manufactured in marketplaces of embodiment: the gym, operating rooms, spas, and so on.

It seems possible that a film like *Fight Club* (*FC*) is responding to the increasing construction of masculinity through discourses of commodity consumption as they are sold to us in pop culture. That is, part of the work of popular culture as a culture industry has been to create pre-existing subject positions for us that categorize bodies into races, genders, body types, sexualities, and so on. These categories are hegemonic, which means two things: First, that there are dominant and predefined sets of ideas about what counts as so-called normal, natural, and commonsensical ways of defining these identities; second, that the stabilization of these ideas as normal is one of the fundamental ways in which society builds what seems to be an entirely normalized infrastructure or what in cultural theory is called superstructure, around the naturalization of a constructed set of systems.

Each of the films and performances documented here and in the next chapter look at the relationship between, in the case of *FC*, popular culture and gender. One of the things that I find completely fascinating about this film, which is itself an example of popular culture, is how it offers a critique of the hegemonic effects of the industry that has produced it (the film). *FC* is the story of a narrator who is nameless (although I'll call him "Ed" to distinguish him from Pitt's Tyler) throughout most of the movie who, upon meeting a second man, Tyler Durden, decides to throw off the lessons of his cultural moment and begin fight clubs, a series of underground secret street-fighting groups where men get together to beat each other up. Ed's character suffers from chronic insomnia and seeks refuge in self-help meetings in which he fakes illness to get "support" and where he also meets Marla. Ed eventually meets Tyler Durden and together they form Project Mayhem, a quasi-fascist activist group that eventually goes completely out of control and wants to bring down the headquarters of all the major credit card companies.

Fight Club represents a particular set of formal challenges to readers of hegemony in popular culture. We are presented with at least two different sets of interpretive options: First, one could argue, although I think unsuccessfully, that this film, which gives us a nameless narrator and main character (Edward Norton's character) and then gives us Tyler Durden, who dominates every scene he is in, shows us how masculinity has been separated from his supposed core essence and is in crisis as a result. What men simply have to do is follow the remedy established by Robert Bly and the anti-feminist men's movement, which is to reclaim their inner warrior and all will be set right. The final thing men must do is to destroy the very things that robbed them of that essence: women and corporate capitalism. However one might be inclined to argue that interpretation, one would have to come to terms with the form of this movie that works violently against such a limited reading. That is, this film is a narrative whose primary form is as, if not more, important than its content. This is a film that not only challenges an easy and unsophisticated reading but arrogantly ridicules that reading as well. In other words, this is a film that refuses realism and its requisite suspension of disbelief by being hyper-aware and very self-reflexive of itself as a representational form, as a film. Recall the several subliminals in the first few minutes of the movie, but also in the self-help group moments where we see several spliced shots of Tyler as he begins to become apparent to Ed. What about the movie title on the marquee outside the movie that Ed Norton stands under? (It was advertising the movie Brad Pitt made after *FC*: *Seven Days in Tibet*) And in addition to several moments of direct address into the camera, we also see the viewer instructed on how to avoid the realism of feature-length films. One of Tyler's jobs was as a projectionist and both Tyler and Ed, in the voice-over, explain how movie reels are changed at the theatre and how Tyler would take advantage of the reel change to insert sexually explicit images into family viewing so fast that no one would really know what they saw. And, at the end of the long flashback that gives us our storyline, Tyler asks Ed Norton's character if he has anything to say and he replies, "Not anything that I can think of" to which Tyler replies "Flashback humour?" Of course, we want to ask why this film, more than many others, is so aware of itself as a film and wants us to be aware of it too. And how does that position its viewers? Why does *FC* want its viewers to be hyper-aware of its fictional status? What, in other words, does it want the viewer to notice about its form and content?

The clue to answering that question is, of course, the unpacking of the trope of insomnia. Recall that Norton's character cannot sleep and moves into a state of hyper-awareness as a result. What does Ed's character say about the effect of his insomnia? "It makes you feel like nothing's real, like it's all like a copy of a copy of a copy." Besides being a direct reference to Baudrillard's notion of the simulacra, to which I will return later, this particular notion of altered consciousness puncturing a hegemonic world view functions as an argument in the film for the social constructedness of not just subjectivity but also reality itself. That is, when hegemony does its job, we no longer notice things about our world that might give us clues to that construction. Insomnia, as something that produces an altered consciousness, becomes one of the ways of beginning to un-know or re-see that construction.

In other words, it stages a crisis of the split subject, a subject produced by as well as being the site of conflict between conflicting hegemonic meanings about masculinity. Ed Norton's character, a.k.a. "Ikea-boy," is not fully present to himself even though he is the proper consumer subject, hailed by all of the hegemonies that construct us in the 20th century, the most fun being "shopping is good" but also that human life can be measured in money and economic value. Recall the scene where his apartment morphs itself into a fully illustrated Ikea catalogue. This is not reality imitating art, it's reality imitating advertising and the hegemonies of commodity culture. Norton takes refuge for his insomnia in the unreal world of self-help discourses, in which he is fully hailed, and through which he's finally able to sleep. And this is precisely what hegemony uses to negotiate our acceptance of its world view: pleasure or what we might think of as a temporary suspension of un-pleasure. Ikea-boy, who also goes by the name Cornelius, Rufus, and "Jack," thinks himself to be fully conscious, rational, and independent until he finds himself sharing the same psyche with Tyler Durden, the overidealized quasi-(anti-authority)-authority/Father figure who represents everything he could never quite be but wishes and attempts, unsuccessfully, to become. "Sooner or later," he argues, "we all become Tyler." Who Tyler eventually becomes is dependent upon an ambivalent identification with but also aggression against these conflicting ways of thinking about masculinity. The entire narrative, after Ikea-boy meets Tyler, spins around these complex hailings. We never really get an answer to his question: "Is Tyler my bad dream or am I his?" although eventually, and again paradoxically, Norton's character can only become himself, that is, enter into discourse, into the "I" of language with a "proper" and fixed name by ambivalently becoming that which he is not: Tyler Durden. Remember that "Norton" is narrating most of this story under duress, in a crisis, with Tyler's "gun" in his mouth? The opening credits visualize this paradoxical *self-other relation* by allowing us to enter the picture through Norton's brain and out the barrel of the gun, foreshadowing the assertion that Norton/Tyler's subjectivity in relation to ideology is our setting.

Finally, recall what Norton does for a living. He works for an insurance company and his "job" is to decide whether to force recalls of dangerous cars or to just pay off those few people who get injured by the faulty cars and not do a major recall; the decision is made by whichever option is cheaper. The narrating "I" of *FC* needs to come to terms with the contradictory ideological legacies bequeathed to him about being a man by various hegemonic institutions: his father (work hard, make money, become your job, etc., vs. Tyler's "You are not the contents of your wallet"); by capitalism; by the police; by his own conscience; by commodity culture; by moral systems (his job) and by the self-help industry. These are the very means through which hegemony works.

This particular argument—that what we think of as the real as well as our own perception of ourselves are both socially constructed—is precisely what *Fight Club* dramatizes. But it also attempts to codify a practice of resistance to this construction and to the anxieties at the heart of what masculinity thinks itself to be. What are these anxieties? If men's bodies are now increasingly in the forefront of cultural and hegemonic scrutiny, what's at stake in this manufacturing of anxieties? If as John Berger states in his book *Ways of Seeing*, that "men watch, while women watch themselves be watched" and that one of the effects of this was, for women, a split and fractured sense of themselves, one that, we might add, capitalism benefits from as women attempt to amend their self-image to bring it in line with that idealized image, then we might be able to argue that the capitalist hegemonic beauty and culture industries have found another market. Masculinity, it seems to me, is similarly fractured as men have an overidealized image of what the most "natural" and therefore most "powerful" man is. If this is true, masculinity is now similarly fractured and willing, so these numbers tell us, to spend a great deal of money attempting to fit the bill as a result.

But where I think *FC* becomes really problematic, of course, is in its remedies for such constructions of masculinity. Instead of becoming fettered in the trappings of femininity and beauty, men need to, or so the film tells us, strip off the trappings of culture to find some rugged and tough iron man within. In other words, it offers an essentialist and almost borderline fascistic notion of identity as an answer to the increasingly socially manufactured nature of masculinity in consumer capitalism. What men need to do is to be "real" men in a land of feminization where women and "minorities" are supposedly to blame for a changing world. And this is where I think the film becomes tremendously conservative and not at all about counter-hegemonic subcultures supposedly outside of the mainstream. So, it is a film filmed with contradictions about beauty, about capitalism, about the commodification of identity, about masculinity and the role of women, as well as contradictions about how to resist these processes.

Of course, *FC* is as essentialist as it is constructivist. It is equally in conversation with the more conservative men's movement as well. And it is in the management of this contradiction that *FC* does, at the same time, predictable ideological work. That is, *FC* is in conversation with the mytho-poetic conservative men's movement, which comes into being through Robert Bly's book, *Iron John: A Book about Men* (1990). Like many of the theorists I have detailed here, Bly also identifies a crisis in masculinity. He suggests that feminism, not primarily but certainly dominantly, has softened masculinity and distanced it from itself. The remedy he proposes is a series of initiations and rituals designed to help men recover a vigorous manhood, both protective and emotionally centred. If masculinity is in crisis, then it needs to do three things: (1) escape from the sphere of the feminine; (2) establish the right relations between men, dictated by correcting the father-wound; and (3) create a space for male affect. This remedy, of course, is guided by the tale of Iron John by the Grimm brothers, which tells a similar narrative.

In many ways, *FC* turns this message from the men's movement into a kind of allegory: *feel your pain* is Tyler's message—not just any pain but physical pain in particular. He also seeks to establish a boy's-only space, one governed by new boy codes. Finally, *FC* also strips the male body free of culture (feminizing) and returns to the iron man inside. While these similarities are undeniable, *FC* and *Iron John* both manipulate this contradiction so as to render its larger message unthinkable. If capitalism and the feminist movement—two relevant examples here, although there certainly could be more—are emasculating men, then this suggests to us that what "men" means is determined by social conditions, not ahistorical biological essences. In both *FC* and *Iron John*, the recourse to a masculine essence is ironic and rhetorical, given the larger hailing to put this inner essence on as remedy to its being chipped away. Either way, masculinity is made by prosthesis and not essence or sexual difference.

Where biological reproduction—one's ability or not depending upon reproduction apparatus—used to be the measure of sexual difference, I am now interested in what I'm calling post-queer genders outside of sexual difference—genders without genitals, to borrow a phrase (Jones, n.p.). This notion argues that gender and sex are now so permanently ruptured that one can no longer be the guarantee of the other. These genders not only matter in the larger scheme of things as I have indicated already, they are genders that defy matter. What they accomplish is twofold: First, they give us pause to look at male masculinity perhaps differently than we have before and, second, they beg the question of to what degree are we beginning to see, in this fertile ground of new affiliations, a rethinking of gender maps, the likes of which was anticipated by Sedgwick when she wrote: "One thing that does emerge with clarity from this complex and contradictory map of sexual and gender definition is that the possible grounds to be found there for alliance and cross-identification among various groups will also be plural" (Sedgwick 1990: 89). Sedgwick is arguing, of course, that the contradictory ways of conceptualizing same-sex desire in the 20th century—as that of either gender transitivity (crossing over genders) or gender separatism (homosocial alliance within one gender)—have complicated histories, but one crucial for understanding gender asymmetry. For instance, within gender separatism, lesbians have looked for identifications and alliances among women in general, including straight women, while gay men might look for them among men in general, including straight men (Sedgwick 1990: 89). Contrarily, under a trope of gender inversion or transitivity, gay men have looked to identify with straight women or with lesbians (on the grounds that some might occupy a similarly liminal position), while lesbians may look to gay men or, as she writes, though this "identification has not been strong since second-wave feminism," with straight men (Sedgwick 1990: 89). To add yet another layer of complexity onto this, with our new trans economies of gender, trans women might look to straight bio-women and to queer femmes (of any gender), but not necessarily to lesbian masculinity, while trans men might look to straight bio-men or sometimes to gay male culture, but not necessarily to bio-lesbians, for affiliation, alliance, and/or recognition of commonality. Sedgwick's argument is bearing most interesting fruit and one of the alliances I want to explore is that between trans men and bio-men, and in particular yet another new gender identity, the boi/boy/boyz.

Such affiliations—and indeed, love, even—between trans men and bio-straight men occurs in the fascinating short film called *Straight Boy Lessons* (Ray Rea). *SBL* is a short montage of black-and-white images sutured together and which, by themselves, make little sense, but they illustrate the larger argument the film is making. In the film, "Ray" is a White working-class FtM who is friends with Bo, another White working-class bio-man. Ray and Bo are an odd couple as friends; Bo's stereotypical position as a White working-class trucker is in direct contradiction with his protective mentoring friendship with Ray and yet it is precisely the similarities—affinities really—in their class and gender that draw them together.

The premise of the filmic moment is that Bo is giving Ray lessons, upon the event of Ray's transition into masculinity, on what it means to be a straight man. As he drives, Bo imparts advice to his newly male companion about how to dress, shave, pick a girlfriend, and act like a man. *SBL*, then, is a visualization of Bhabha's prosthetic: the images show us masculinity grooming and dressing, but we also see action figures playing as part of a culture of boyhood. These are the signifiers of masculinity that are as significant to Ray as a carefully constructed male body. They do not accrue "naturally" to that body; they are cultivated, learned, and worn like clothing. Bo's instructions in the voice-over are equally significant. Bo passes on 13 lessons in manhood to Ray, the most significant of which are "as a White guy, everything is your fault. Get used to it." On the one hand, it might be possible to read Bo's argument as a kind of dismissal. But, in conjunction with other lessons that, in essence, teach one how to relate better to women, how to dress and groom, etc., this is the remaking of conscious manhood. This film is also a testament to the political changes in manhood, coming from the least likely and most contradictory source, the truck-driving, working-class, self-identified White trash, Bo.

I am interested in theorizing the possibility of affiliation between these two unlikely men as an example, but certainly look for it, admittedly, in what might initially seem like all the wrong places. I am less interested, in other words, in actually mapping the field(s) that this book is situated in (either queer studies or trans studies or sexuality studies or masculinity studies, etc.) and just want to play in these fields a bit. I want to ask universalizing (in Sedgwick's sense of that term) questions about what might happen if we widen the circumference of two terms: man and the boy, or masculinity and the trans boy, to suggest that the former (manhood) is finding its self in an imaginary reconfiguration of the latter (boy). That is, instead of arguing who is inside or outside of these categorical imperatives, or over what counts ontologically as a boy, I want to play with these categories to see how my subject—transed boyhood—might look differently if we look for it where we are not suppose to find it: on, for lack of a better term, bio-heterosexual masculinity. The larger stakes? To ignore this particular site of trans masculinity or trans subjectivity is to give credence to the argument that the contours of the body are determined by flesh rather than by discourse and signification. If we cannot deny or disavow masculinity, as Bhabha suggests, then we can—within the larger ideological and discursive economies of essentialism, racism, and heteronormativity— disturb or trouble its manifest destiny, and deny, at the very least, its invisibility. By drawing attention to masculinity as a free-floating signifier, we rearticulate it, again to quote Bhabha, as a prosthetic subject. Bhabha uses the notion of masculinity as prosthesis—a "prefixing" of the rules of gender and sexuality to cloak or hide a lack-in-being—to denaturalize the masculine and to frustrate its articulations. Thus, the topic of this chapter is not necessarily the trans-gendered boy as we've known him—that is, away from the male body, where Halberstam tells us we might find him as the FtM boy, or the butch boy, or the tranny-boy—but as the prosthetic bio-boy, as in, for instance, Tyler, Cornelius, and Bo as well as Ray. I am looking here for the trans-gendered boy because if Nietzsche (1968: 355) was right when he argued that "what is familiar is what we are used to and what we are used to is most difficult to know," than I want to argue that boyhood where we think we know it best—on biologically male bodies—is actually the thing that we need to unknow, to see as estranged, distant, alienated if our queer, trans-sexual/trans-gendered, and even feminist politics are to succeed.

Lest this seems completely far off the field, let me recall some recent moments where popular culture is engaged in a similar project of rewriting masculinity through the trope of the boy, beginning with the obvious: the list of boy bands seems to double every few years. The first generation may have included many of the early Motown all-boy groups; it might have also included the Beatles, the Monkees, or later still, the Jackson Five or the Osmond Brothers. Given my definition of a boy band—that is, as an all-boy group who puts on display in performance the boy body and boy-subjectivity as uniquely different from adult manhood—we might at least agree that within these terms, the first-generation boy bands had to have been the Bay City Rollers, Wham!, New Kids on the Block, and Munedo. Once pop music became acceptable again, our second generation was dominated first by the Backstreet Boys and 'N Sync. The third generation came quickly on their heels: O-Town, SoulDecision, 3 Deep, 98 Degrees, 64-4, Boyz II Men, Ricky Martin, Savage Garden, Boyzone, and so on. Boyhood in music is big business and these boys are outselling everyone. The Backstreet Boys alone sold 1.1 million copies of their *Millennium* CD in the first week of its release. Their stiffest competition in terms of numbers comes from other boy bands who, for all intents and purposes, are impossible to differentiate from each other.

To be sure, these are some of the boyz of music; what about other popular culture forms? In film, is there a tranny-boy who was not stunned by Halley-Joel Osmond's eternal plea to the blue fairy in Spielberg's *AI* to "make me a real boy"? Or a man who wasn't both fascinated and horrified by the boyish desires of Buck in the stunning if not a little creepy *Chuck and Buck*? Recall that Brad Pitt and Ed Norton played a similar dynamic in *Fight Club*, which opens with the narrator imagining that his special friend has his gun in his mouth; recall earlier that Durden seems to name what the film/novel imagines as the sentiment of a generation of disaffected men: "We are an entire generation of men, raised by women," to which Ed Norton replies, "Yes, I am a 30-year-old boy." It could even be argued that Hilary Swank won her Academy Award for acting *across* gender lines in *Boys Don't Cry*, something that might seem so unthinkable to non-drag-king-friendly audiences that it was perceived as *uber*-acting at its best. Regardless, Swank and director Kimberly Pierce brought Brandon Teena back to us as an extraordinarily beautiful young boy. More boys at the movies? *Spider Man* turns the superhero back into a boy. *Sixth Sense*, *American Beauty*, and *Monster's Ball* all depict the inner torment of boys who know what adult manhood can't possibly know about itself (that the Fathers, as they have known themselves, are dead). *Monster's Ball* in particular was fascinating. In many ways, and from the point of view of Hank, Billy Bob Thornton's character, the movie seemed to be about the impossible choice between White patriarchal southern American manhood, as embodied by Hank's father, Buck, and a nostalgic, imaginary boyhood. This story is set in Georgia where the prison-industrial complex has inherited southern racist values and economics from slavery. All of the men in this family are prison guards. Hank has two options as the film opens: coffee and ice cream—that is, become his White, racist, southern patriarch father, Buck, or become his son, Sonny, the soft, southern boy who attempts to look forward in the history of race relations in the South and not backwards. The catch is that that son cannot exist as a real son. Hank, in other words, has to murder his son in order to become him in the end. Even more movies about magical boyhood: *Harry Potter*, *Lord of the Rings*, and the two *Star Wars* featuring new boy actors in each film. And beyond movies, lest we forget, it will be a boy, rightfully or wrongfully, who leads the British Royal family into a new phase of its history. Since the death of Princess Diana, the international tabloid circuit, including American magazines like *People*, simply cannot get enough of princes William and Harry.

Why this obsession with the boy? Is this just simply a case of an emerging economic demographic (youth culture) or is there more than what can be accounted for through reductionist economics? It may well be partially due to this age group, but demographics beg the question of what it is that makes a boy a boy and not a man in the first place. Is a boy decidedly chronological? Not according to MuchMusic's boy band quasi-drag king show *2-Get-Her*. This half-hour spoof of both boy bands and the popular ABC show *Making the Band*, the reality television show that documented the process by which O-Town came into existence, suggests that boyishness is not at all about age. One of the members of their boy band is bald and appears to be in his 40s. The contradictions between his behaviour and his age foreground boy subjectivity as anything but age. He is as young, cute, goofy, soft/non-phallic, and as appealing to the band's fans as any other member of the group.

So, if age is not the thing that makes a boy a boy, what is? In his chapter, "Why Boys Are Not Men," Steven Cohan searches for answers to these questions by looking at the history of boys and men in Hollywood, suggesting that the boy first appeared in the films and film cultures surrounding the new 1950s boys of Hollywood (*Masked Men*, 1997). Tracing the emergence of what tough-guy John Wayne dubbed the "trembling, torn T-shirt types"—Marlon Brando, Montgomery Clift, James Dean, Sal Mineo, the young Paul Newman, etc.—through the postwar era, Cohan posits that Hollywood crystallized a new boy-man. "One has only to recall," argues Cohan, "the galvanizing early screen appearances of the young Clift and Brando to see how readily imagery of a youthful male body, not only beautiful to behold but also highly theatricalized, marked out the erotic appeal of these new young actors within the star system, underscoring their alienation from the screen's more traditional representations of masculinity" (Cohan 1997: 203). What appealed to mainstream American culture was precisely this notion of boyishness. Such a new look challenged the conflation of sexuality and gender that supported a symbolic economy in which "boys" were made legible and thinkable as the opposite of "men." The result of this open rejection of the imperatives of masculinity (i.e., grow up and be a "real" man) was an erotic performance or impersonation that productively always fell short of the original. In falling short—that is, in refusing to be all that a man was suppose to be—the boy brings himself into existence as a viable male subject.

Moreover, what was particularly compelling about the boy was signalled by Wayne's adjective "trembling." The term rightly suggested a conflation of that "new look" with an emotionality and vulnerability. Whereas old-guard actors like John Wayne embodied virility and hyper-manhood, stars like Brando and Dean interiorized masculinity, converting social nonconformity and rebelliousness into inner torment and emotional excess. Where Wayne-esque Hollywood he-men wore masculinity on the outside as action, toughness, and phallic power, the Brando and Dean types resisted such exteriorizations of masculinity in favour of a look synonymous with failed manhood: perpetual boyhood. The boy, then, became a positively gender-conflicted concept that at once signified failed masculinity and an excess of masculinity, disturbing the ease with which Hollywood's men equated sexual potency with hyper-masculinity.

Kimberly Peirce and Hilary Swank's depiction of Brandon in *Boys Don't Cry*, for instance, both relies on and outs the queerness of the Hollywood boy. Rather than suggest that the boy has simply failed in his gender, it is much more productive to suggest that these failures, in fact, are evidence of the theatricalization and, hence, denaturalization of the boy. Is not part of the appeal of boyishness precisely its masculine feminization? In other words, I think part of the appeal of boyishness is its promise of phallic power and its resistance of its masculinist heteronormative imperatives. This was something articulated in the early days of the feminist men's movement by Stoltenberg. The appeal of the boy is not necessarily a confusion of gender, but the potential for its refusal of the teleological imperatives of manhood. And this is precisely where this instance of masculine feminization overlaps with female masculinity: Boys paradoxically threaten to become men while categorically rarely materializing and, more often than not, refusing that identity outright. Peirce herself locates Brandon as a Frankensteinian boy within this history of Hollywood's No Man's Land:

In addition to representing a queer archetype, Brandon actually embodied many traits of the traditional Hollywood hero. He had the innocence and tenderness of Montgomery Clift in *Red River* or a young Henry Fonda, the naive determination of Jimmy Stewart. He was a rebellious outsider like James Dean, a shy, courtly gentleman around women like Gary Cooper .... Bringing Brandon to Hollywood was like bringing him home.

Such a precise reading of Brandon situates him within the realms of those historical performances and within contemporary reiterations of that genealogy, evident in the "new" new boys of culture.

One boy in particular has held my interest for some time now and, I would argue, gives us some information about what kind of imaginary or ideological work the boy is doing even if we can only skirt around the ontological questions. If you watch television or go to the movies, you cannot help but have noticed the Mazda "Zoom-Zoom" commercial featuring Mika. You will recall that "Zoom-Zoom" is the copyrighted tag line of the Mazda car company. Developed by Mazda Australia's advertising company in a collaboration agreement with the Mazda U.S. agency, Mazda's commercial introduces us to 12-year-old boy Mika, dressed in a boy's suit, turning to face directly into the camera and whispering "zoom, zoom" while a voice-over asks, "What would happen if an SUV was raised by a family of sports cars?" Answer: A vehicle that is transed: "An SUV with the soul of sports car," introducing us to the all-new mini-van/SUV Tribute, which weaves in and out of a pack of Miatas, learning from its sporty siblings by imitating or copying their every move. At the end of the commercial, the Tribute veers off onto a dirt road, emphatically highlighting its SUV credentials, while the entire time a world-music beat articulates the images and the car metonymically as the desirous Other. Could there be a more potent trans metaphor of masculinity? This articulation, of course, brings to mind Dionne Brand's argument that the cultural productions of people of colour—that is, expressions, gestures, understandings, dress, aesthetic tastes and sensibilities, music, and so on— are taken up and used as creative backdrop to multinational markets (Brand 2001: 51). While I cannot find evidence that the tag "Zoom-Zoom" itself is such an expression, the music that makes "Zoom-Zoom" work certainly is recognizably Other to the whiteness signified both on the screen and hailed in its viewer. In some ads, especially the version of this commercial shown in movie theatres, special effects of a sneakered foot on a skateboard or riding a BMX bicycle superimposed over a similar foot pressing on the accelerator of the car/SUV reiterate what Mika articulates visually. That is, that this vehicle—

what is essentially a mini-van—will wake men up from their engendered adult amnesia by reminding them of that which they had to forget in order to become grown-up men: the pleasures of boyhood.

These pleasures—driving fun, Mika, and boyhood motion—are all evidence, I would argue, of this new trans-masculine imaginary in popular culture being articulated through the trope of the boy. When masculinity unknowingly and anxiously asks, "What is my I?" increasingly these are offered by capitalism as answers: prosthetic stylization that implies but is no longer dependent upon male corporeality; boyish "Zoom-Zoom" play in commodity capitalism; and the nostalgic deferral of "real" adult manhood to an elsewhere in the "real" world. French theorist Jean Baudrillard anticipated this postmodern imaginary economy when he wrote about Disneyland as a perfect model of the simulacra (1995). Recall that Baudrillard theorizes the simulacra as the liquidation of the real, where signs of that real come to stand in for the real itself. The simulacra is the condition of postmodernity where the tenuous distinction between the true and the imaginary, the real and the "false" dissolves. All are unreal imaginary; all referentials, things that we imagine to be real, have been emptied of content and origins, and then, at the same time, have been artificially resurrected in systems of signs. This is not a question of imitations or copies of the real, but is instead copies of the idea of originals. This new hyper-real is no longer reducible to the distinction between the real and the imaginary but is itself a phantasmagorical generation of an imaginary unreal without origins or reality.

Baudrillard calls this hyper-real the simulacra, but he also uses the phrase a "Disneyland imaginary," which, I would argue, works by analogy to account for the televisual and Hollywood film apparatus that this chapter references. "Disneyland" (or later what he calls imaginary stations that feed reality) are a perfect model for "all the entangled orders of simulation." It is the play of illusions and phantasms, but more importantly this imaginary is conditioned by what he calls the enchantment, or what Louis Althusser called the interpellation of the crowd into this imaginary and ideological apparatus (1971). However, it is with this crowd or viewer that the imaginary station does its most effective ideological work and that is to disguise a third-order simulation that is not so immediately obvious: Disneyland (television, the Hollywood movie apparatus, and so on) or other imaginary stations like it are there to conceal the fact that they themselves are the "real" country and that all of "real" America is Disneyland; they are presented, in other words, as imaginary in order to make us believe that the rest is real when in fact all of the rest of America is no longer real but of the order of the hyper-real and simulacrum. Is it not, therefore, a question of this Mazda commercial, or the boy bands, or Disney, functioning as false representations of true reality that is then consumed by "real" subjects but rather the opposite? It seems to me that these simulations conceal the fact that the real itself is no longer what we used to think it was (if in fact it ever was). Thus, the Disneyland imaginary, or what I call this boyish masculine imaginary, is neither true nor false, but instead functions similarly to reverse the fiction of the real. In other words, it masks the assertion that, in this case, neither the boy in the commercial nor the interpellated man-boy viewer are real; both are unreal; both exist in and as a prosthetic hyper-real imaginary. For the implications of this I return to Baudrillard, who argues that one of the meta-signs of the liquidation of the real by the simulacra is the infantalizing, degenerative identity of this imaginary. "It produces," he suggests, " an infantile world, [where] the adults are elsewhere [where power is elsewhere] in the 'real' world … childishness is everything, particularly amongst those adults who go [to Disneyland] in the first place" (355). I would add here: Hence the prosthetic and similarly unreal "reality" of masculinity. What's put on here, what comes to stand in as a prosthetic fiction of the real, is a trans-performative reformation of masculinity through this nostalgic trope of the interiorized boy. Masculinity thus becomes itself through a rearticulation of boyhood, which adult manhood is unknowingly suppose to leave behind. If this is true, then masculinity is anxiously transed, not in terms of gender difference, but in terms of age. Quite literally, we have masculinity imagining that it finds its present self in a fiction of its past self, not between boyhood and manhood, but by folding manhood back into boyhood, so that "real" manhood exists in that Disney-esque elsewhere. Is this why we see Jeep answer Mazda in their new commercial? Recall in this commercial we now see man-boy Ethan (from "Survivor: Africa"), head down, counting, playing hide-and-seek with his friends, only now the setting is a (hyper-)reality televisual imaginary where rainforests, mountains, and islands are the playground of these transed and hyper-real boys. Is this not then prosthetic masculinity in drag, not performing across gender necessarily, but in a hyper-real, nostalgic, and transed fantasy of boy-ness?

By way of conclusion, let me just raise three very short points about the cultural work the boy is doing, points I explore in upcoming chapters. First, this prosthetic performative trope of the boy and/or boyhood is the discursive point of overlap between heterosexual masculinity, drag kinging, and tranny, and lesbian-boy cultures. I will consider drag kinging performances of boyhood in my next chapter, but this work is also arguing for a new set of (admittedly sometimes ambivalent) alliances of the type imagined by Sedgwick when she argues that shifting our terms can open up space across different subjects or across No Man's Land. Again, it's curious that Judith Halberstam continues to make the argument that masculinity is anything but theatrical and prosthetic, and why, to a lesser degree, her work on drag kinging doesn't explore the popularity of the boy as a persona among drag kings.

Second, not all boys are created equal. "Boy" is a term with a long history of violence within White supremacy. Not every subject will inhabit this free-floating signifier equally; while "boy" might be appealing, even potentially interventionist (albeit ambivalently) for White masculinity, the term has always functioned as a tool of violence within the history of White supremacy—that is, within economies of White supremacy, for Black masculinity, manhood, and blackness have always been rendered incommensurate. I am not entirely sure that the boy will necessarily have equal kinds of political currency at every moment to each materialization of masculinity, but that said, one of the strategies that I will consider in the next chapter on drag kinging is the use of the term "boi" in hip hop cultures where resignification through alternative spellings flags what Butler (1993: 224) calls a Nietzschian "sign-chain," where the history of a custom or word can be a continuous chain of ever new meanings and interpretations. These resignifications—sign-chains—are what Bakhtin identified as the dialogisms of language in lived contexts. One of the central premises of Bakhtin's work is the parallel between the construction of texts and the construction of the self. Both centripetal (stabilizing uses of language and meaning) and centrifugal (uses of language that destabilize meaning, allowing for resignifications) forces intersect through a term like "boy," which is not the product of a closed system but of social acts or "active participant[s]" that respond to and anticipate other utterances (Bakhtin 1981: 233). As we have seen already, Bakhtin's concern rests with language as living speech in its concrete totality (what he means by "discourse"), he suggests that the meaning of any linguistic sign is diachronic and relational, involving different speakers and their use of words within sentences. The lesson from Bakhtin suggests that if language is inseparable from its specific socio-historical context, then protocols and liabilities tenaciously persist: "Language acquires life and historically evolves [...] in concrete verbal communication, and not in the abstract linguistic system of language forms" (Bakhtin and Medvedev 1978: 129). The results of these context-determined utterances are meaning-making processes dependent upon contexts. Language as discourse is productive, and relations of language evoke present, past, and possible future contexts as well. Thus, it follows that the constitutive nature of a word like "boy" itself embodies a multiplicity of meanings and traces of its past usages.

"Boy" and "queer" are words, sets of ideological liabilities, sets of protocols even, increasingly their own box marked by so many "intense sideward glance(s)"—both toward racist histories—that each is becoming a term that marks everything and by implication, absolutely nothing at all (Bakhtin 1984). But where I want to call for a post-queer language economics, the gendering and, even more so, racial histories of the term "boi/boy" as a sign-chain seem to remain productively refractable. Wesley Crichlow's (2004: 15) groundbreaking work, *Buller Men Batty Bwoys: Hidden Men in Toronto and Halifax Black Communities*, makes a similar argument about the term "bwoys" in that it functions as a complicated index of sexuality, even if it sometimes does so with negative as much as productive connotations. That said, it still remains significant that not all boyz, bois, boys, or bwoys share the same relationship to language, to power, and to the teleological imperatives of heteronormative manhood, making precision and context-specific self-naming all the more critical.

And, finally, where is this "adult elsewhere" to which "boy" defers? If you've seen the "Zoom-Zoom" commercial, you will have noticed for the briefest of seconds a young, White, blonde girl who is on the screen very briefly and whose hair flies up as this boy-in-motion zooms past her. She looks about the same age as Mika, although she looks decidedly more grownup than he does. Similarly, does not Hermione in *Harry Potter* resonate a kind of grown-up-ness that Harry lacks? It seems to me that femininity, especially these "grown-up" little girls, are now standing in as the elsewhere that boy-ness defers to from the edges of manhood. In Chapter 5 I will return to such deferrals and articulations of femininity.

NOTE

1.   As indicated earlier, language is not a transparent form. When one changes the spelling of particular words, one foregrounds the representational functions of language and the way in which language mediates our relationships to "reality." The different spelling of words like, for instance, boi, indicates an ironic relationship to both the signifier, boy, but also to the categorical meanings, signifieds. Boi is to boy, then, what femme is to femininity.

Chapter 3

BOY TO THE POWER OF THREE:
TORONTO'S DRAG KINGS

LET ME MAKE A CONFESSION AT THE OUTSET: I LOVE DRAG KINGS. I AM what you might call an academic fan of drag kings. I saw my first drag king show on June 29, 1995, when the Greater Toronto Drag King Society staged a "Drag King Invasion I," at a Toronto drag bar called El Convento Rico to an audience of about 600 screaming fans. It was quite a ride that night and, then, as an out lesbian, it was beyond just about anything else I had seen before. The performers were equal parts campy, sexy, outrageous, raucous, and utterly tenacious. The crowd was whipped into a kind of queer frenzy, and in a bar designed for drag queen performances, lesbian public cultures were permanently transformed.

This chapter will explore those transformations through three different waves of drag kinging in one major urban centre: Toronto. I borrow the wave metaphor from feminism and find it useful to characterize three different historical moments in the evolution of drag king cultures in Toronto. These are not easily characterized as generations; age ranges may not differ dramatically between groups and some kings travel comfortably between each wave, mentoring young generations of upcoming kings. But what is significant about these waves is the social, historical, and epistemological context that each maps. The first wave—the Greater Toronto Drag King Society—is easily situated in but not of lesbian performance contexts, such as those mapped by lesbian performance theorists, Jill Dolan, Kate Davy, and Sue-Ellen Case. Even as these drag king performances challenge the work of the lesbian theorists, historically this first wave overlaps with changes each notes in the development of a body of literature on lesbian performances, such as those of the WOW Café and the performances of Lois Weaver and Peggy Shaw of Split Britches. Drag kings do not fit easily into the work of Dolan, Davy, and Case, but are significant in the sense that they begin to mark the rupturing of lesbian discourse, theory, and identity by what I call the butch-femme renaissance. This first wave of kings in Toronto begins to expand the circles around "lesbian" to map an imbrication with the then emerging queer theory and nation.

The second wave—The Fabulous Toronto Drag Kings—emerge, as waves do, at the end of the first wave. With the emergence of this troupe, drag kings are dis-identified with lesbian cultures even though they perform in lesbian contexts. What begins to emerge instead is an entirely different set of relationships marked by affiliations with both gay masculinity and trans masculinities. Where the first wave engaged in mimicry of masculinity, the second wave begins to complicate that mimicry through an increasing identification with masculinity and dis-identification with exclusively lesbian subject positions. I trace those identifications, dis-identifications, and the ways that a second wave begins to foreground a consciousness of race, especially of whiteness, into performances. Finally, I explore the work of one king in particular, Deb Pearce, and hir alter ego, Man Murray.

Finally, after the dissolution of the Fabulous Toronto Drag Kings, which overlaps with the emergence of a third wave that includes a variety of groups, including Big Daddy Kings and United Kingdom, and then with a fast fourth wave, Bois Will Be Boys and KingSize Kings—what I will develop as "bois to the power of three"—discernible gender identifications and affiliations are all but rendered incoherent. What exists instead are both self-referential (performances that signal the representational practices of the first wave and earlier lesbian cultures) and a plethora of gender identities off known gender maps. These are productively incoherent genders in No Man's Land. Moreover, what makes each wave newish, in addition to the existence of a new group of performers, is also physical performance space as discursive as well as geographical location, particularly bars in a large urban centre like Toronto, where different neighbourhoods with varying demographics lend each wave an entirely different character through its fan base.

One of the things that links these waves together, even through some pretty significant differences, is their proximity to discourses of masculinity and a dependence on this larger problematic for their condition of possibility. While not every performer identifies with masculinity, even the dis-identifications mark a persistent relation to larger, cultural scripts of gender. As Butler told us in 1990:

> The "I" who would oppose its construction is always in some sense drawing from that construction to articulate its opposition; further, the "I" draws what is called its agency in part through being implicated in the very relations of power that it seeks to oppose. To be implicated in the relations of power, indeed, enabled by the relations of power that "I" opposes is not, as a consequence, to be reducible to their existing forms. (Butler 1990: 123)

She reminds us that thinking in excess of social construction renders any subject, and masculinity in particular, incommensurate with self-knowledge or unable to know that which makes it it/self. Self-consciousness, in other words, is not in and of itself the remedy as consciousness is conditioned by language and is a product of language at the same time. Curiously, then, it's often what the subject cannot know just yet that conditions what it can know. Two points here: First, these configurations of our sense of self are always ambivalent, that is, configured around what we think we know even as we are aware that there is more to a self than what ego knows about itself. Second, more remains leftover, then, undefined and these are the things which animate the self we do think we know. Drag kings draw out this ambivalence and stage it for both pleasure and parody. The work I want to do with drag kings is located at the meeting point of these ambivalent contradictions and paradoxes, a space I am hailing as yet another No Man's Land. If we cannot deny or disavow masculinity, as Bhabha suggests we cannot, then we can, within the larger ideological and discursive economies of essentialism, racism, and heteronormativity, disturb or trouble its manifest destiny, deny, at the very least, its invisibility. By drawing attention to masculinity as a free-floating signifier, we rearticulate it, again to quote Bhabha, as prosthesis, "prefixing" the rules of gender and sexuality.

AT THE BUTCH-FEMME LESBIAN BAR: DRAG KING INVASIONS

First, I want to situate my reading of the "Drag King Invasion I" as lesbian cultural production at the crossing of "performativity and the loose cluster of theatrical practices, relations and traditions known as performance," and more precisely for my purposes here, "lesbian theatre" (Parker and Sedgwick 1995: 1). The tension between performativity and performance fuels the erotic intensity of the drag king show. In other words, the tension or ambiguity between the so-called "reality" of the performance—its parody of the "hyper-masculine star" at his most contradictory and illusory "stardom" as a technology of desire, and performativity or the identificatory processes themselves—marked the show that night as an important and pleasurable event.

Second, my reading of the show foregrounds the axiomatic, discursive, and historical slippage between the terms "camp" and "drag." On one axis of my rather oppositional taxonomy rests earlier lesbian feminist "performance" theorists Kate Davy, Jill Dolan, and Sue-Ellen Case, focusing on the woman-run performance spaces Split Britches and the WOW ("Women's One World") Café. To conflate the arguments of these three theorists would be a mistake; however, they not only share similar questions, they anticipate issues foregrounded in theories of performativity, and provide a lens through which I want to read the drag king show. Those are: the problematization of the field of representation itself; an interrogation of reading practices vis-à-vis performer-audience dynamics, and, finally, the outing of butch-femme subjectivities as constitutive of a "lesbian aesthetic." As Kathleen Martindale (1996: 32) suggested, much of this early work held high hopes for articulating a radical and political aesthetic. "While the utopian appeal of such anti-realist hopes for aesthetic activism is compelling ... even the critics most responsible for producing these determinist readings concerning the new lesbian spectatorial communities came to acknowledge that they hadn't paid enough attention to the contradictions within discourses and within spectators" (Martindale 1996: 30). Nonetheless I agree with Martindale's assertion that the demands on lesbian avant-garde writing/performance art for political accountability can be traced back to early feminist theory and practice, so I will set the stage by revisiting that work. I will return to those "contradictions both within discourses and within spectators" a bit later. Kate Davy attempts to discern an essential difference between what she identifies as gay Camp and a lesbian performance aesthetic. In her "Fe/Male Impersonation," Davy disparages what she identifies as the misogyny inherent in Camp, arguing that it not only says "something about women" to the men it is intended for, but it effaces women in the process. Moreover, Davy suggests gay Camp doesn't translate on the "lesbian" stage as Camp is driven by "a fierce masculine-feminine heterogendering," which cannot work for a lesbian aesthetic. Finally, Davy begins the outing of butch-femme subjectivities as a solution to the problems posed by male impersonation. Defined in opposition to female-to-male cross-dressing, butch-femme doesn't "hide the lesbian beneath" and as such "dismantles the construction of woman ... challenges male sexuality ... [and] challenges the heterosexual contract" (Davy 1994: 145). In other words, butch-femme as the motor of lesbian performance is "lethal" (Davy 1994: 145).

Jill Dolan is also concerned with the field of representation itself and the reading of lesbian theatre—that is, with the relations between the performer and the reader/spectator. In "'Lesbian' Subjectivity in Realism: Dragging at the Margins of Structure and Ideology," Dolan (1990: 42) eschews realism as a strategy of representation, arguing that realism offers "unhappy positionalities for lesbians ... the ideological inflections of which are crucial to mark." One of the inflections that Dolan marks is not only the denial of butch-femme generally, but the feminization of the butch herself.

> By the mid-1970s, the sexual lesbian who engaged in butch behavior as a subcultural resistance to the dominant culture's gender and sexual ideology was silenced by feminism, her transgressive sexual desire "femininized" through the woman-identification that neatly elided active sexuality as a pre-condition for lesbianism. (Dolan 1990: 49)

In "The Discourse of Feminisms: The Spectator and Representation," Dolan goes on to theorize the position of the individual spectator and spectorial communities in the making of a specifically "lesbian" desire in representation. While Dolan posits a rather unitary and White spectator undifferentiated by class, gender, and race, she attempts to rethink the argument by film theorists Mulvey, de Lauretis, and Doan, which suggests that the series of "looks" built into the structure of film position the male spectator as subject and woman as the passive object of the male subject's active desire. Dolan too deploys butch-femme in a rhetorical move that anticipates Butler's notion of "citationality," arguing that butch-femme "quotes" gender to appropriate the male gaze for the purpose of "looking" and "reading" queerly both in the theatre and in the performance of the everyday as well.

> The drag role requires the performer to quote the accepted conventions of gender behavior. A woman playing a man ... is quoting gender ideology, holding it up for critique .... When the assumed gender role does not coincide with the performer's biological sex, the fictions of gender are highlighted. (Dolan 1988: 116)

Finally, Sue-Ellen Case herself fully outs the butch-femme couple as the definitive subject positions in not just lesbian theatre, but in feminist theory as well. Paradoxically nodding in two directions at once, both through feminism and against feminism, Case's "Toward a Butch-Femme Aesthetic" attempts to resolve a theoretical impasse in thinking to date (circa 1988) about the lesbian subject. Case is in conversation with Teresa de Lauretis, who argued in "The Technology of Gender" that the female subject is already trapped within the concept of "sexual difference," either a biologically overdetermined "female subject" or evacuated significatory effect. De Lauretis interrogates the limitations of both positions and offers another perspective—again, from the "space-off"—that concept term borrowed from film theory, which identifies the space not visible in the representational frame but inferable from what that frame makes visible. This space is where we find the terms of a new perspective that will allow the "subject of feminism" to move between "the (represented) discursive space of the positions made available by hegemonic discourses and the ... elsewhere of those discourses," at once both inside and outside of ideology (de Lauretis 1997: 26). In a very clever rhetorical move, it is within the "elsewhere" of de Lauretis's own "subject of feminism" that Case finds her dynamic duo, the butch-femme couple.

> The butch-femme subject could inhabit that discursive position [where] the female body, the male gaze, and the structures of realism function as only sex toys .... In recuperating the space of seduction, the butch-femme couple can, through their own agency, move through a field of symbols, like tiptoeing through the two lips (as Irigaray would have us believe), playfully inhabiting the camp space of irony and wit, free from biological determinism, elitist essentialism, and the heterosexist cleavage of sexual difference. Surely, here is a couple the feminist subject might perceive as useful to join. (Case 1993: 305)

As Bob Wallace (1996: 98) notes, the other axis—"performativity"—as signified in the last decade by "queer theory" generally and Judith Butler in particular, answers that of performance and its attendant identity politics by suggesting that all identity categories are performatives or acts of signifying systems that gain efficacy through stylized repetition. Gender is no longer an immutable and natural "fact" waiting for articulation in discourse, but is a fictional and discursive effect of signifying systems. Moreover, Butler's work problematizes the distinction between "sex" and "gender" as it was read in feminist theory. If the two are no longer suggestive of a biology vs. culture split as feminism argued, then logically, to quote Butler (1990: 6), "man and masculine might just as easily signify a female body as a male one, and feminine a male body as easily as a female one." Thus, while *Gender Trouble* suggests that gendered performances such as butch-femme are not pathological imitations of heterosexuality, but rather are a kind of fictional imitation for which there is no original, Butler's next work, *Bodies That Matter*, through its interrogation of "sex," suggests that it too is fantasy, the effect of the reiterative regulatory sexual regimes (Butler 1993: 15). Thus,

> If gender is the social construction of sex, and if there is no access to this "sex" except by means of its construction, then it appears not only that

sex is absorbed by gender, but that "sex" becomes something like a fiction, perhaps a fantasy, retroactively installed at a prelinguistic site to which there is no direct access. (Butler 1993: 5)

While much of the work by the former lesbian performance theorists is very much grounded in its own historical moment—lesbian-feminism with its attendant essentialisms—this body of work attempts to map a kind of "performative," which Butler polished in her later and highly influential works. I suggest that the interrogation of "performance," as very tentatively mapped by Davy, Dolan, and Case, can be reconstituted as the three lenses through which to read the work of this early wave of drag kings: first, butch-femme in its 1990s manifestation as parody of a recognizably lesbian signifying system and heterosexual gender roles; second, the function of an audience or authorizing witness for such performances/performatives; and third, lesbian drag in its proximity to larger technologies of heterosexuality.

An impossibility structures this citation of the performative event at the Toronto bar that night, indeed in any live performance. Peggy Phelan notes that nostalgia, or "the wound of wishing to return," structures any attempt to report, record, or repeat that performative.

> ... even at the seemingly simple level of the linguistic sign it is impossible for writers to convey the complete context in which a[n] ... act occurs. To report it back, to record and repeat it, is at once to transform it *and* to fuel the desire for its mimetic return .... Much of the writing [about performatives] is a record of a living relation between the writer and the artists she sees. This seeing is, necessarily, a distortion, a dream, a hallucination; writing rights it back toward reason by creating enabling fictions .... The effort to "cite" the performance that interests us even as it disappears is much like the effort to find the word to say what we mean. It cannot be done. (Phelan 1993a: 19–22)

That night I remembered a range of mostly White masculinities staged in performance: Andy Gibb; John Denver and Placido Domingo; The Village People; Billy the Kid or other Nashville or Hollywood cowboys; Freddie Mercury; Guns N' Roses' Axl Rose and guitar player Slash; and Anne Murray herself. What underwrites these performances of masculine "stardom" as well as the conventional live music show is how each "star" signifies beyond just a "genre" of music. Each constructs gendered subject positions, types of physicality, identities, fashions, in other words, *star texts*, intertextual constructs produced across a range of often contradictory media and cultural practices (as quoted in Gledhill 1991: xiv). In other words, each of these signifiers signals entirely different identitarian as well as musical discourses: disco (Gibb and The Village People); country ("Trouble"); folk (Denver); rock (Freddie and Axl); and whatever descriptor we might use to characterize the *star text* loosely organized around "Anne Murray."

What intrigued me about these performances was the obviously contradictory and at times hysterical visualization of the tensions of masculinity as a heteronormative discourse. Contrary to Davy's assertion (1994: n.p.) that male impersonation does not "say anything about men" other than their erasure of women, I suggest that male impersonation speaks volumes about masculinity. But I do think Davy is right that we need to learn to read lesbian drag differently, and I offer the following very tentative speculations about that reading paradigm. The drag kings' performance suggested to me that lesbian drag, as opposed to Camp, might depend not so much upon excess or an excessive send-off of heterosexual masculinity, but upon equivalency instead. To put this into other terms, if we define mimicry as "the parodic hyperbolization of a gender identity," and masquerade as "the nonironic or unconscious assumption of that identity," then it seems this dyke drag show did not spin around mimicry's distance from masquerade but rather upon its approximation to it instead. The drag kings' mimetic act takes masquerade, or the unconscious assumption of identity, as its object (Fuss 1995: 146). In other words, in targeting masculinity as a supposedly "natural" identity, the show simultaneously signalled both process and product, unveiling performance technologies, with "technology" both as a discourse naturalizing identity categories as well as the illusion-producing apparatus of the theatre/stage itself, and the performative or the fictive identities produced. While gay Camp foregrounds the performativity and excess of traditional femininity through its over-the-top parody, masculinity remains unmarked and underspoken. The drag kings foreground that cloaked status, and parody masculinity's own unspoken artifice, even though, as Butler (1990: 235) rather paradoxically suggests, "[a woman performing masculinity] is perform[ing] a little less, given that femininity is often cast as the spectacular gender." Moreover, it seems that Davy was both right and wrong—right in that male impersonation puts a different spin on its object than gay Camp, but wrong in that lesbian performance, at least in this particular manifestation in this moment, is as implicated in a "masculine-feminine heterogendering" as gay Camp.

Moreover, part of what this male impersonation speaks about masculinity is its contradictions and inevitable and thus repetitive failures. As Butler

(1993: 231) suggests, "to the extent that gender is an assignment, it is an assignment which is never quite carried out according to expectation," where the addressee never quite inhabits the ideal s/he is compelled to approximate. In their parody of heteronormative masculinity as "failure," the drag kings flesh out Butler's assertion. For instance, the drag kings seem quite fond of hijacking musical acts that rely on either duets (Donny and Marie Osmond, John Denver and Placido Domingo) or groups (The Village People). The duet as a music convention is a form just asking for "trouble." And troubled it was. One of the most raucous points of the show that night occurred during the Domingo/Denver duet when, at the big climactic end of the song, John and Placido could no long hold back, and commenced necking onstage. Similarly, as Axl Rose and his guitar player Slash finish flailing around on stage, Slash falls to his knees and gives Axl a rather enthusiastic blow job. While seeming to be great fun for most folks in the audience, including the gay male waiters and bar staff working that night, these particular performances foregrounded and parodied masculinity's hysterical fear of "feminization" *vis-à-vis* sexual desire between men.

Furthermore, the drag kings' impersonation of masculinity and parody of sexual desire between men relies on but also shifts away from what Case identified as the butch-femme couple and toward what I have identified earlier as a continuum of female masculinity. Evoking those axiomatic epistemological tensions outlined by Sedgwick in *Epistemology of the Closet*, that same-sex desire is understood either as an expression of the essence of one gender (gender-separatism) or as cross-gendering (gender transitivity), what overdetermines the male impersonation at the heart of the drag kings' show is a shift from the separatist to transitive trope, complete with its shifts in alliances and cross-identification. To quote Sedgwick (1990: 89), "under a gender-separatist [trope], lesbians have looked for identifications and alliances among women in general [while under] ... a [trope] of gender [transitivity] ... lesbians have analogously looked to identify with gay men, or, though this latter identification has not been strong since second-wave feminism, with straight men." Clearly, the drag kings' performance could be grouped under gender transitivity and the proliferation of butch-femme subjectivities as anticipated by Case. (We will see later in the second and third waves that it is precisely this dynamic that these latter waves tease out; that is, there is a decided move away from lesbian affiliations toward ones with masculinity instead.) But fuelled by its referent "butch-femme of the 1950s," or Case's butch-femme couple, butch-femme of the 1990s will, as I will argue a bit later, in many ways far surpasses its own history, demonstrated by the proliferation of female masculinity in all its complexities: FtM trans-sexuality, butch-bottoms, soft butches, butchy-femmes, stone butch, fag butch, etc. Subsequently, the masculinities performed on the stage signify in very contradictory but remarkably rich ways, simultaneously as "butch," and in excess of "butch," an approximation of heterosexual masculinity, and an outing, queering, and poaching of that masculinity as well.

Elspeth Probyn (1995: 81) reminds us, in her essay "Lesbians in Space," to think about the question of human geography or, more precisely, the fact that bodies exist in relation to other bodies within socio-spatial sites as well. And the space of the performance that night was a queer bar, not a theatre. If I were to limit my definition of "stage" to what it was that we all supposedly looked at, then it would be difficult to go much further than discussing the kings on stage. But I want to suggest that we read the "stage" as the front door of the bar instead. The drag kings' performances do not take place in isolation; the audience, especially but not exclusively its femme audience, is as much a part of the performance as those in the spotlight. In fact, I would suggest that audience, or femme desire, is the central condition of the performance (Wallace 1996: 102). The audience, or at least the many panties that land on the stage, are props in the performance as much as the performers are in the show staged by the audience. But this contingent authorizing and contingent community is not made up of Dolan's undifferentiated, unitary subject. Nor is it Mulvey's passive female subject, the object of a masculine gaze. Rather, this was an audience made up of as many desiring and identifying boys and girls, actively reading against the grain of hegemonic gender and desire, desiring and authorizing not just the complex performances "on stage," but reading and read by the many other performances "off-stage" as well. Thus, what is staged and negotiated is not "lesbian identity" as ontology, but the beginnings of a very queer and eventually post-queer desire as it's constructed through the multiple identificatory and dis-identificatory positions opened up through and across the performances in that bar as a queer space. Identifications within and across the show as performative event constitute its seductiveness, not ontologies (Hart 1993: 131).

If Butler is correct, as Lynda Hart suggests, that the power of lesbian subjectivity may be not in appearance but in disappearance, in "letting that which cannot fully appear ... persist in its disruptive promise," then the drag king show that night was doubly potent (Butler 1991: 29; Hart 1993: 134). The remarkable irony of the event was that, unlike the performances of Split Britches and WOW Café, this show did not have one single "Lesbian" on stage, short of Anne Murray, of course. Needless to say, there were lesbians performing both in, to, and around the bar. Indeed, "lesbian" was the defining condition of the show. But I suggest that this was a very different performance of "lesbians in space" than the realist, "positive-images" school of lesbian representational politics. That apparitional creature, the Lesbian, lurked continually in de Lauretis's "space-off" just outside of view, and no matter how hard one worked to catch a glimpse of her, she remained productively absent. The drag kings engage gender as "an inevitable fabrication," working gender against both identity and heteronormativity, staging, not "representing," lesbian desire.

I have been suggesting that a reading of the Toronto drag king show through the enhanced lens offered by performance theorists Davy, Dolan, and Case, as well as Butler's complex and rigorous theories of performativity, can layer the drag kings' queer performances of masculinity. What seems to be at stake in both bodies of work is, as Butler (1993: 233) notes, an "increasing politicization of theatricality." What Davy, Dolan, and Case remind us is that such an increasing politicization has an important set of both performance and epistemological histories.

LONG LIVE THE QUEER KINGS: THE FABULOUS TORONTO DRAG KINGS

Where the "Drag King Invasion I" suggested that heterosexual masculinity doesn't quite hold together, the Fabulous Toronto Drag Kings demonstrate that White masculinity doesn't always cohere together either. The Fabulous kings, later known as The Toronto Drag Kings, held court in Toronto for the last half of the 1990s. Produced by Clare Smyth ("Flare"), also a drag king performer, both the Fabulous and Toronto Drag Kings became a standard feature in the Toronto queer, lesbian, and performance scenes for over seven years. This wave, made up of a fairly consistent group of performers—Flare, Zach, Stu, Deb Pearce ("Dirk Diggler" and "Man Murray"), Jesse James Bondage, Christopher Noelle, Chris, Moner, and Mitch[1]—introduced Toronto to some of the most innovative and long-lasting king performances around. This was also the first group to represent Toronto in the International Drag King Extravaganza, in Columbus, Ohio, October 1999, and many of these same kings—Dirk, Christopher Noelle, and Flare—have developed a kind of notoriety that has bumped them to a national level. For instance, Flare and Christopher Noelle appeared on *Queer as Folk*; Jesse James Bondage, Flare, and Dirk all appeared on the *Maury Povich Show*; and Christopher Noelle appeared in the Toronto Unity 2000 show with rock star Cyndi Lauper.

What this next wave of drag kings articulate in their performances is as vast and unique as the kings themselves. Themes include ironic spins on famous duets or groups; interesting or hyper-masculine characters from popular culture; famous musicians or artists; some, like the performances of Jesse James Bondage, perform songs that have had meaning at various points in time (especially popular are songs from a king's high school years). Other kings, like Mitch, imitate famous artists known for their genre-specific style or dance moves. As I discuss below in more detail, some kings emulated their favourite bands while others again, like Man Murray, impersonate famous Canadian icons rumoured to have queer histories (Anne Murray). While this group presented literally hundreds of performance scenarios, there are a few consistent tropes that I want to draw out here.

First, a stock favourite of a number of these kings are the places where masculinity, especially White masculinity, speaks volumes about itself in very ironic ways. That is, of course, through race and the operations of White supremacy. As I suggest in Chapter 4, if one of the key elements of whiteness is that it disavows itself as a racialized identity, standing instead as *the* human race, as universal mankind, then a consciousness of race and the processes of racialization start becoming one of standard features of the second wave of kings. Two of the White kings in this troupe target precisely that paradoxical hyper-visibility and yet invisibility of whiteness: Zach does an impressive angry young White boy in his salute to *Rage against the Machine*. What makes this particularly effective is that Zach wears an "Anti-racism Action" t-shirt that shows a young White boy jumping up and down on top of a swastika. The effect is to mark whiteness from inside and articulate it against the invisibility of White supremacy. Moner too stages whiteness as a subjectivity simultaneously hyper-visible and invisible. Moner performs a song called "Pretty Fly (for a White Guy)." The lyrics of this song document the ways that White masculinity imagines itself in relation to men of colour, who are read as "hip" and "cool." "Our subject," so the lyrics tell us, "is not cool but fakes it." He dresses up, overcompensates to fit the part and to disguise the emptiness of whiteness: he listens to the "right" music (Vanilla Ice), cruises in a cool car (a Pinto), and tries "too hard" to imitate his fantasy of Black masculinity. The song inverts a White racist gaze back at itself, and shows whiteness to be both vacuous and hyperbolic. Moner's version of this song forces attention onto the artificiality of the White subject in the song and denaturalizes and makes that artifice even more ironic. As Moner said to me in conversation, "It's important to work the White boy persona—that's what I am." Whiteness is marked and articulated—that is, made to work by revealing itself. If you think about the verb to articulate, it means to divide into words, to pronounce or utter. But it also means to connect or mark with joints—that is, to be connected with sections. Thus, to articulate is to express fluently and to manipulate a site where component parts join (as in a knee or hip), to bring segmented parts together to enable functionality. These kings dissemble White masculinity, break it into parts, and then reassemble those parts to make them work differently, to render them dysfunctional. If White supremacy works best when it's hyper-visible and invisible, it cannot work in quite the same way when it is denaturalized, rearticulated, and, most importantly, de-cloaked.

In the same way that whiteness manifests itself and speaks through normative masculinity, gender is also spoken loudly through a queering of heteronormative male sexuality. A number of the kings stage the sexual failures at the heart of straight masculinity. For instance, during a number where Kelly, Flare, and Zach dress down to look like stereotypical ill-kempt, working-class men with huge beer bellies and perform "I Am Too Sexy," the men at one point drop their pants to show their butts to the audience. Two of the three are wearing men's underwear, which is what you might expect. But Flare's character is wearing girl's panties and subsequently gets chased off the stage for it. Chris and Stu do a similar routine, only their characters are hyper-masculine soccer players; one player (Stu) has a crush on the other (Chris) who at first refuses him, but then who returns his advances and finally carries him off the stage. The song is the "Cup of Life" by Mr. Contradiction himself, Ricky Martin. Ricky represents an entirely curious figure of masculinity. He's racially marked, but sings in English; he's hypersexualized as a man of colour, but that oversexualization is always already overdetermined as simultaneously in excess of heteronormative masculinity. What's parodied in these numbers is the sometimes very thin line between gay and heterosexual masculinity, where queer and ironic reading practices articulate the contradictions that masculinity often disavows and yet is unable to contain. The first wave of drag kings in Toronto similarly played with these tensions. Not to be outdone by the "original" Village People and their own parody of gay masculinity, the Fabulous Toronto Drag Kings' Village People parodies a parody in a performance that simultaneously signifies masculinity, hyper-masculinity, failed heteronormative masculinity, and White notions of queer diversity all at the same time (Photo 1). This wave of drag kings-staged queer community when Flare, dressed in a sailor suit, performed Kermit the Frog's "Rainbow Song" while the rest of the kings joined him on stage with rainbow flags in a group finale (Photos 2a and 2b).

Photo 1: Fabulous Toronto Drag Kings. Village People.

Moreover, the drag kings' mimicry of masculinity and parody of sexual desire between men relies on but also shifts away from what we might identify as butch-femme sexual identities toward a continuum of female masculinity, and then off the map completely to what I will call "something a wee bit different." What better ground to map that difference onto but the female masculinity as an open secret coded onto Canadian singer, Anne Murray. Deb Pearce's Man Murray has been a stock and, clearly a beloved, feature of almost every drag king wave to date. What makes Man so pleasurable is how Deb's performance codes not just irony but layers of irony onto each other. Layering refers to the way that drag kings will map a king persona onto their own gender identities, allowing that identity to show through cracks in the mapping (Halberstam 1998a: 260). Deb draws our attention to Anne Murray's own layering of identity. Murray has long been rumoured to have a lesbian past; this rumour is virtually unverifiable. But what is far more interesting about this rumour is the degree to which it is fed by a disavowed spectre of masculinity around Murray's gender identity, including her deep baritone voice. Despite the signifiers of femininity that accrue around Murray—makeup including the requisite blue eye shadow, earrings, long gowns, feminine pantsuits, women's low-heeled shoes, and so forth—her performance of White femininity always seems to fail given it is layered onto a body that reads more masculine than feminine. That is, one could argue that Murray herself, as text, reads as a very toned-down male-to-female drag queen (Photo 3).

Photo 2a, 2b: Flare as Sailor. Photographs by Bobby Noble.

It is precisely these already existing ironic layerings around Murray that Man Murray foregrounds. In performance, Man wears a rainbow flag dress which replaces the evening gown, but many of the other markers seem consistent with the codes around Anne Murray: the short, masculine hairstyle, square jaw, broad face and smile, strong hand tightly gripping the microphone in a fist; pantsuits with slip-on shoes, step dancing where she moves awkwardly from side to side, etc. What makes this performance so effective—that is, what makes the irony so resonant—are the similar facial features that Anne Murray and Deb Pearce share, especially evident in Photo 4. This is the face of White butch masculinity, accompanied by what for me, as a young teenage butch, was unequivocally the voice of female masculinity as well. How else might we characterize that deep baritone voice? Only for Anne Murray, femininity is layered—albeit unsuccessfully—onto female masculinity. But Man, of course, is not just layered, he's also queerly camped up. Man is packing a phallus not unlike the microphone Murray grips so tightly; Man draws out the awkwardness of body movements, dancing centred at the knees as they step from side to side, giving equally awkward facial expressions (the wink, complete with blue eye shadow and head nod, for instance); and inhabiting Murray's body through favourite songs, such as "Snow Bird."

Clearly, such ironic and simultaneous reiterations of failed heteronormative femininity, disavowed female masculinity, and queered gay masculinity

Photo 3: Anne Murray.

return us to Sedgwick's axiomatic epistemological contradictions and to a post-queer No Man's Land. What overdetermines the male impersonation at the heart of the drag kings' show, such as Man Murray, is a shift from the separatist to transitive trope, complete with its shifts in alliances and cross-identifications (Sedgewick 1990: 89). In many ways, I think this latter turn toward masculinity has finally been taken. Christopher Noelle, for instance, plays on the different expectations between looking like a girl and identifying as a boy in his number "Sharp Dressed Man." Noelle comes out in a tight, black, slinky dress with hair down and proceeds to transform himself into a John Travolta-looking man (from *Grease*) in front of a mirror on stage to the song "Sharp-Dressed Man." The transformation from femininity into masculinity in some ways defies the premise I began with—that is, that femininity is about hyperbole, masculinity about understatement. Noelle puts on the man using as many accessories and props as he takes off. And Chris too (formerly Ricky Martin in the "Cup of Life"), who returns to do "Livin' La Vida Loca" Ricky Martin, also references this turn when he tells me "I am the straight man of the lesbians .... It's hard for me to do the gay stuff on stage." Moner and Jesse also do a song, "Mr. Roboto" by Styx, which rearticulates these identifications with straight men. The narrator of the song is a self-made man, who allegorizes the natural and ultimately defamiliarizes the liberal humanist "man": "I have a secret I have been hiding under my skin … I am not what you think / Forget what you know / I am the modern man who hides behind a man so no one else can see my true identity." Clearly, the drag kings' performance could be grouped under the category of gender transitivity and the proliferation of butch-femme subjectivities. But fuelled by its referent "butch-femme of the 1950s," female masculinity of the 1990s in many ways far surpasses its own history, demonstrated by the proliferation of female and male masculinity in all their complexities: trans man, straight man, butch boy, butch-bottoms, soft butches, stone masculinity, gay masculinity, fag butch, etc.

Photo 4: Deb Pearce. Photograph
by Dominic Chan. Kind courtesy
of Gay Guide Toronto.

Curiously, these rearticulations and performative deconstructions of masculinity are very telling of these affiliations with masculinity and dis-identifications with lesbian practices and identifiers. For instance, I asked nine of the kings one day if they identified or found themselves at all in the word "lesbian." All nine of them said no, including the one self-identified femme; they offered me a bevy of other words, but not one of them said "lesbian," suggesting that the history of lesbian politics has been both incredibly successful and a failure all at the same time. Barbara Johnson anticipated this kind of paradox when she wrote on the failure of success:

If the political impulse of [lesbianism and/or queer theory and/or performativity] is to retain its vital, subversive edge, we must become ignorant of it again and again. It is only by forgetting what we know how to do, by setting aside the thoughts that have most changed us, that those thoughts and that knowledge can go on doing what a surprise encounter with otherness should do, that is, lay bare some hint of an ignorance one never knew one had. (Johnson 1987: 16)

In other words, if irony is less about controlled self-consciousness and about its failure instead, then these scenes of irony needs to be read for what they reveal about ourselves and our identifications. To phrase this differently, what drag kings do is stage the things that whiteness and masculinity do not want to know and cannot know about themselves, to use irony to make these subjects strange and make their ambivalences work against what they think they do know. As a mode of critical politics, the scene of irony has to be inherently noisy and dialogic in the Bakhtinian sense—that is, that it is engaged in many conversations all at the same time. As a discursive mode of the unsaid and the unseen, irony is the ideal form in which to stage ambivalences, ambiguities, and contradictions. Meaning is made and confused, reduced and complex all at the same time. Drag king performances are both inherently dialogic, in conversation with both conservative and oppositional politics of gender, with lesbian feminism, queer theory, homophobia, feminism, with race and racism, with trans-gendered politics, etc., but also with the contradictions that fracture each. Irony troubles correspondences; it removes certainty that we mean what we say or, conversely, that reality is somehow reducible to some appearances. It also betrays the continuous and inevitable failure of the visual as an epistemological mode.

In addition to my arguments that: (1) drag kinging allows for the ironic rearticulations of whiteness and masculinity, especially of those things they cannot know about itself, and (2) that the culture of drag kings produces— indeed, necessitates—new affiliations across gender and sexual orientations, my own interest as of late has been in those performances of more abjected masculinities: the guys who perform, for lack of a better term (and I use this term affectionately) "pond scum." I remember listening to a friend talk once about a king character she was creating and developing. In her non-drag king life, she's one of the best-looking, most charming gentleman butches around: "He" she said, referring to her drag persona, "is nothing but pure pond scum .... He's gross to women. He's entirely flirtatious in a way that is completely disgusting. He's constantly grabbing himself and making those offensive noises to women. He's a pig!" How might we begin to make sense of these somewhat paradoxical articulations of a kind of masculinity that, 15 years ago, we might have tried to intimidate into disappearing? What are the pleasures of watching, say, "Jay," who did a similarly stunning non-musical performance in which he impersonated an incredibly homophobic man who picks up what he thinks is a woman in a fag bar, has sex with her, then, upon discovering she was a drag queen, beats her up. Jay held his audience spellbound while he performed this scene. The larger question at stake in a performance like Jay's is similar to one articulated earlier by Hall. Hall (1996: 143) rereads Bakhtin to ask the question: "Why is it that the thing we deem socially peripheral ... be[comes] symbolically central?" Why did Jay's character, a homophobic man, hold us spellbound that night in a dyke bar? Part of my answer lies in reformulating the question to ask what cultural work the category of drag kings does. My tentative answer is that when drag kinging emerged, it worked toward articulating an unspoken tension inherent in identity politics that continually asks what we are. Our political task must be not finding out what we are, but understanding the relations between what we say we are and what we deny we are. I am not implying that female or trans masculinities are actually Mr. Pond Scum at their core. But I do want to suggest that the power of the drag kings lies in their exposure of the impurity of categorization itself, especially those categories that have historically understood themselves to be bound, distinct, somehow discrete, and separate (like, for instance, our history of lesbian separatism and, for some of us, the history of White supremacy). These lines that are crossed are there to differentiate, say, lesbian from straight man, Black from White, but that line already allows "in" that which it is suppose to "ward off." It binds identities in the very same gesture through which it supposedly differentiates itself. By way of a conclusion, I suggest that the drag kings remind us, with Bakhtin (1981: 91), that: "When one finds a word, one finds it already inhabited ... there is no access to one's own personal ultimate word ... every thought, feeling, experience must be refracted through the medium of someone else's discourse, someone else's style, someone else's manner ... almost no word is without its intense sideward glance at someone else's." If this is true of words, then, of course, it must be true of our identity categories at the same time.

KINGS TO THE POWER OF THREE: BOIS WILL BE BOYS

With this third, and likely by now even fourth or fifth, wave of kings the proliferations of gendered subject positions move beyond "something a wee bit different" into something unrecognizable on our gender maps. Curiously, though, one of the stock features of continuing waves of kings is the presence of the boy. This boi—as either a lesbian boi, gay boi, or FtM boi—is an exceedingly popular trope performing either solo or with other boys (and hence the title of one of these new troupes, Bois Will Be Boys). Why is it that the boy bands—or, if not actual boy bands, then acts or performers that foreground *boyishness*—are such popular fodder for drag kings? Here in Toronto, as recently as 2003, several new boy acts appeared on the drag king scene, including the utterly compelling trans trio/*ménage-à-trois* New Cocks on the Block. But the *boy* has featured as a stock choice in drag king numbers—at least here in Toronto—for as long as drag kings have been performing. The New Cocks on the Block are a case in point: their 2003 appearance at the bar formerly known as Pope Joan signalled a new turn in the Toronto drag king scene where several incarnations of the boy converged. The event at a lesbian bar was a convergence of those who, across a spectrum of subjects, might identify with the term "boi": butch bois, lesbian bois, trans bois, the tranny-fag-boi, gay bois, and, judging by the demographics of the huge audience, the bio-boy (admittedly, in some instances, dragged out by their girlfriends for a night on the town, or so several of my straight female students later confessed).

If, as I suggested in Chapter 2, we agree that this boy is theatricalized and, by implication, denaturalized, soft, always stylized, and anti-heteronormative in his orientation to the imperatives of masculinity, then could we also agree, perhaps, that whether he appears on stage in a lesbian bar or in a fag bathhouse, or in a (bio-)boy band, this subject is always trans-gendered? As I suggested in Chapter 2, the Brando and Dean types resisted such exteriorizations of masculinity evident in the "new" boys of culture: Leonardo di Caprio or the more numerous boy bands. These teen idols and objects of teenage girl fandom and consumption are sexualized through a feminizing gaze that is seductively threatened by the very thing boys supposedly lack: phallic power.

But one of the crucial triangulations that I am also seeing in this new wave is the way in which the figure of the boy/boi functions as a hybrid, anti-essentialist hinge point between three different kinds of resisting masculinities: lesbian boi, trans-sexual boi, and drag king bois. This figure remakes manhood and gives us new vocabularies that are not just anti-essentializing but simultaneously a-essentialist; that is, they draw our attention to the ways that we remake gender every day as fiction through our reading practices and our desires. But even as we attempt to remake gender as a fiction, these fictions are still heavily and sometimes violently regulated with heteronormative cultures. One of the results of that regulation is, of course, a particular relationship to cultural and political, and hence public trauma. Ann Cvetkovich's new book, *An Archive of Feeling: Trauma, Sexuality, and Lesbian Public Cultures*, argues a curious relation between trauma, sexuality, and public cultural production by suggesting that both power and trauma are productive rather than repressive. Unhappy with increasingly commodified self-help approaches to trauma, as well as with theories of trauma that overly individualize and decontextualize trauma from its socio-political frameworks, Cvetkovich provides a theoretical framework within which to theorize the role of trauma in the production of what she calls queer counter-cultural publics. I do not want to get lost in theories of trauma at this juncture, nor am I suggesting at all that drag kings are working out private traumas on the stage. This has always been an accusation levelled against queers, trans-folks, gays, lesbians, bisexuals, etc.—that is, that somehow these queer and resisting subjects are a traumatic response to and interruption of heterosexual identity. That is not at all what I am arguing here, nor is it what Cvetkovich is suggesting either, but I do think it is necessary to draw our attention to a couple of axioms of queer theory and activism about trauma as they inform the performance cultures of female and trans masculinities. First, it is still traumatizing, both individually and culturally, to live under any of these signs of difference. Whether it be "queer" or "lesbian" (two signs that I will not posit here as mutually exclusive) or "gay" or "transed," and despite the many social and political gains made, it is still a traumatizing everyday experience to be different, although, of course, the everyday experience that I detail here is always mitigated by power *vis-à-vis* race, class, ability, ethnicity, nationality, and so forth. Moreover, both trauma and queer cultures have been marked by an unspeakability or unrepresentability in public cultures; both have had to aggressively insert themselves into the public domain, but each has also had to struggle to preserve histories and spaces (Cvetkovich 2003: 8). Each has been marked by a permanent tension between "official" and "unofficial" narratives or knowledges; each has found/created languages in a kind of ironic or unconscious rearticulation of public/heteronormative languages. Finally, as Cvetkovich (2003: 7–8) herself notes, the memories of each have been embedded not just in narratives but also in material artifacts, which can range from photographs to objects whose meanings might seem arbitrary but for the fact that they are invested with a particular kind of value.

Quite apart from specificities of individual traumas (bashings, sexual abuse, loss, and so on), Cvetkovich posits what a number of other queer theorists, including Sedgwick and Butler, have and that is that social and political traumas give rise to counter-cultural public spaces. But Cvetkovich (2003: 18) takes this one step further and it is this argument that interests me in terms of drag king cultures: she particularizes these relationships to argue that if trauma presents an epistemological challenge, standing at the crossroads of the complex relation between knowing and not knowing, then it can be a particularly potent discourse with which to "sort through the everyday relation between categories rather than resolve them." Cvetkovich (2003: 20) puts it this way: "I am interested instead in the way trauma digs itself in at the level of the everyday, and in the incommensurability of large-scale events and the ongoing material details of experience .... I hope to seize authority over trauma discourses from medical and scientific discourse in order to place it back in the hands of those who make culture, as well as to forge new models for how affective life can serve as the foundation for public but counter-cultural archive as well."

One of the things that continues to be brilliantly reiterated in the performance of the New Cocks on the Block/KingSize Kings are the traumas of living in these incoherent bodies around which I centre a post-queer politic. I want to end this chapter on drag kings with their work because in the few performances I have seen, they struck a chord with me in how they staged a resistance to their traumas on the site of gendered bodies. As I noted much earlier in this chapter, the return to previously viewed performance art is structured by what Peggy Phelan identifies as a kind of nostalgia, or the wound of wishing to return (1993c). These performances are ones I return to because in many ways, they overlap with many of my own experiences with an identity in transit. For me, as a trans person, two sets of surgeries occurred during my last few years in Toronto: breast-reduction surgery and chest-reconstruction surgery. The butch body and the FtM body are each marked by different relationships to trauma: the first, at least in my experience, carried a profound ambivalence to breasts, while the second alleviated the first, but was not itself without traumas. The first performance I saw by New Cocks on the Blocks staged these bodies in trauma and in sometimes ambivalent transit. Two of the then original three performers of New Cocks came on stage with their chests wrapped in what was supposed to be the surgical tape used after breast reconstruction. Under that see-through material, drawn in red on their breasts, were bright red lines, again mirroring the incisions made to reduce breast size. At this point, not that long after my own surgery, I am not even sure I noted the song they performed, but I certainly made note of the trajectory of the performance. In the beginning of the performance they treated their chests as sites of wounding, but when the number came to a close, they had dramatically removed the see-through bandage and the red incisions, and celebrated their breasts. The message of the number was a clear refusal of the traumatizing interventions of breast reduction and removal. These are three very queer, young, non-operative trans-gendered youth with very unconventional bodies who, as part of a new trans wave, clearly seize authority over traumatized incoherent bodies from medical and scientific discourse in order to place those bodies back in the hands of those who make culture with them instead. They are not only bodies of incoherence, they are also, quite literally, bodies on the line, embodying new possibilities for resistance.

NOTE

1. Names are a curious thing with drag kings. Many have at least two, their birth names and at least one character name. Given that drag kings are part of a queer community, not all drag kings are comfortable using their full legal names. For clarity, I will identify kings primarily through their character names, although I will often use full names if I have received permission to do that. Some names

mark a character or persona performed by a king while others might mark a trans identity taken on by the king and then, by extension, performed on stage. Character names, of course, are far more interesting given the way in which irony is built into them. Some names are spins on popular characters from Hollywood movies (for instance, Dirk Diggler is from the movie, *Boogie Nights*; Man Murray references the Canadian singer Anne Murray), while others are ironic spins either on a birth name or character trait or popular identity. Names are an important feature of the performance long before a single king steps onto a stage. Moreover, many kings do identify as trans, but many do not, identifying themselves as butch, queer, gay, or, in some cases, femme or feminine.

Chapter 4

OUR BODIES ARE NOT OURSELVES: TRANNY GUYS AND THE RACIALIZED CLASS POLITICS OF INCOHERENCE

That was when I realized a shocking thing. I couldn't become a man without becoming The Man. Even if I didn't want to.

— Jeffrey Eugenides (2002: 518)

IN MY FIRST DEPARTMENT MEETING AS A PROFESSOR AT YORK University, one held during the CUPE strike on our campus in 2000, the department was attempting to address the gender imbalance among its rank of full professors. Given that many of the full professors are male, the department was taking the very important step of finding a remedy to this situation. One senior professor (but not full professor), a woman who teaches, among other things, feminist literature, made the very curious claim that given how easy it is these days to change one's gender—and this even after the Ontario government de-listed sex-reassignment surgeries—that she would volunteer to do so if it would allow her to access the pay increase that accompanied a full professorship. A round of laughter ensued in which all seemingly agreed that this was indeed an easy process and the meeting continued. I sat a little dumbfounded that—in the midst of the CUPE 3903 union labour action on the campus, a local that has been remarkably progressive in its inclusion of trans issues in its mandate, and in the face of the aggressive de-listing of sex-reassignment procedures *and* the sad reality that male full professors still outranked the females—any of these matters would be so easily the source of laughter among faculty. This work is addressed to, in part, not only the female professor in question but to those folks inside of feminism who might claim that trans is not a feminist issue.

As I have been suggesting so far, issues around the prefix *trans-* present not only theoretical but lived opportunities to refine our intersectional reading practices. The perspective I want to explore here is one that will allow us to see trans issues as not only those of gender but also those of race and class as well. The titles of two significant feminist books on class—Dorothy Allison's *Skin* and bell hooks's *Where We Stand*—signal the precise articulation I want to explore here: that between (trans-)[1] embodiment, class, and labour. Each text argues, among other things, that materializing class within feminist theoretical paradigms is often accomplished through corporeal metaphors. Moreover, each also suggests to us that class, the one term within our intersectional frameworks that is often neglected, is itself perceived to be about a kind of hyper-embodiment and hyper-visibility, especially for those of us who are working class and racialized White. If the anti-racist field of whiteness studies is correct, as I will argue later it is, then being classed as White is whiteness racialized as visible, especially since whiteness operates through ironic codes of invisibility and, hence, epistemological and discursive power. That is, whiteness comes into visibility as whiteness when it is articulated through class. If that is true, then under what conditions can transed bodies, bodies that similarly matter when invisible and/or fetishized, emerge within the feminist analytical intersections of capitalism, class, and race? I want to play in those fields by offering my own trans body—which is White but formerly off-White,[2] formerly lesbian but now female-to-male trans-sexual—as a case study in resistance. A practice of strategically unmaking the self—that is, working the labour of self-making against the categorical imperative—is a class, trans, anti-racist, and union politic I want to cultivate in this era where "self" is the hottest and most insidious capitalist commodity.[3]

The union motto that I want to borrow—an injury to one is an injury to all— has been in my life since I was very young.[4] My maternal grandmother was a member of CUPE for her entire working life; she was a hospital worker when services, like laundry and food, were still provided in-house. She worked in a hospital laundry for almost 40 years. I spent one summer as a young teenager working in that same laundry with her and just barely lasted the first month. Conditions were horrific. Unpacking the laundry from the hospital hampers was one of the nastiest jobs I have ever witnessed. Thankfully, I suppose, the staff wouldn't let me near the job of separating soiled sheets, bloodied towels from the operating rooms, and so on. Temperatures were extremely high and dangerous. Between massive pressing machines that ironed linens and sheets, the huge dryers, and washers that laundered sheets at very high temperatures, workers were dehydrated on a regular basis. After working for 40 years in daily conditions like these, my grandmother was given a CUPE ring that I still have and wear on a chain around my neck. I remember visiting her on her lunch break when I was much younger; I would wait for her in the hospital cafeteria and when the laundry women came into the room, they certainly were quite a sight. Into that otherwise unremarkably populated cafeteria walked a group of White, working-class, big, tough-looking, often hard-drinking women dressed in white dress-uniforms that looked out of place on them. They lumbered into the cafeteria, lit cigarettes, opened their homemade lunches, and stared down all who dared to look. Those women, a formidable bunch of working-class women who were literally at the bottom of the health-services industry but upon whom it depended, made a mark on me. Much later when I walked the CUPE 3903 picket line at York University with my teaching assistants as a new faculty member, something of those early workers infused my determination to see that strike through to its conclusion. I doubt that much of CUPE 3903's current work on trans-sexual issues would have made much sense to those women with whom my grandmother worked, although I suspect a couple of them might have understood the stakes. Because of the political commitment to social justice issues, CUPE 3903 has passed a number of resolutions that include the struggles of trans-sexual peoples into their primary mandate. They also support their trans-sexual members with funding; when I had surgery, CUPE 3903's Ways and Means fund helped me pay for a procedure that has been de-listed in the Conservatives' butchery of Ontario health care.[5]

The men in my family were less union-affiliated but just as affected by the class-based issues of labour activism. My grandfather was one of the "Little Immigrants," groups of White, working-class, orphaned British children shipped to Canada from the homes of Thomas John Barnardo, a philanthropist in 19th-century London, England. Thomas Barnardo, along with others, established a series of reformatory and industrial schools known as "ragged schools" (because of the ragged clothing of the attendees) for homeless and abandoned children. In the 19th century, they struck a deal with the Canadian government whereby they would export large numbers of these children to Canada to work as "farm" help and "mother's helpers" in Canadian homes and farms (Bagnall 1990: 91). At its peak, this emigration was responsible for shipping between 80,000 and 100,000 (orphaned or abandoned) children to Canada, a ready-made, exploitable "servant" class (Bagnell 1990: 9). Most of these children, now known as the Barnardo kids, would end up working as indentured domestic servants. My grandfather was one of those who came to Canada via Montreal in 1916 as a young boy to be adopted into a farm family, or so he thought. Instead, he lived in the barn, was ill fed, beaten, and overworked until he was old enough to run away. He did, and set up a life for himself in Canada as a labourer, eventually marrying my grandmother in northern Ontario. As one of the students of a ragged school, my grandfather was still unable to read and write when he died in 1992.

About one thing I felt certain: these were the primary influences on my gender. My grandfather had an entirely ambivalent relationship with England:

I suspect he had always felt abandoned and banished from it, although as a young boy from a very poor family, he had already lived the life of an exile on the streets of London. He remained vehemently class-identified and anti-British for his entire life, continuously evoking cultural traces of England and, unknowingly, its particular form of class whiteness while constantly disparaging both at the same time. I find traces of both grandparents in the words I use to describe myself ("a guy who is half lesbian") and, in finding these traces, have built a sense of self quite different from their own. The rough and yet somehow vulnerable masculinity of the butches and FtMs brings my grandmother back to me, while, in some kind of temporal and geographical displacement, I find traces of my grandfather's off-whiteness in the class-based traces of manhood I now wear as corporeal signifiers.

To be sure, my family and I are all White. When I say "off-White," I do not mean to suggest at all that somehow being poor and/or working class means that one is no longer White. What I mean is that whiteness, like gender and class, has a history of invention, construction, and utility. Embedded in those histories are the processes that manufacture whiteness in the service of modern nation building. I was reminded of this when I watched the film, *Gangs of New York* (2002). For all of its problems, the least of which is its final ideological return to pre-September 11 United States *vis-à-vis* images of the World Trade Center's twin towers, *GONY* depicts the simultaneous whitening of Irish immigrants and the utilitarian invention of the nation-state. The thing that renders the "tribal" or "gang" conflict inconsequential, in the final scenes of the film, is the intervention of the American government through its military.[6] Through its need to govern a people, the United States government first had to invent them. This, of course, occurs long before the timeline represented in the film, but the film is an allegory of the process whereby certain groups of light-skinned immigrants into the "Americas" purchased their way into White citizenry. Amsterdam (Leonardo di Caprio) and Bill the Butcher (Daniel Day-Lewis) are equally made subject to the American government and can become just plain American men (code for American White men) because they have what James Baldwin referred to as the price of the ticket.

If racialized bodies are the product of both our own labour and the work of a racial social manufacturing machine, then developing not just a tolerance for, but an acquired taste, for destabilizing paradoxes within our feminist vocabularies might be one way to trouble that machinery. Female-to-male trans-sexuals embody but are also articulated by paradox: Loren Cameron's (1996) photographs in *Body Alchemy*, to which I will return in my afterword, visually represent this paradox. The guys whom Cameron photographs, especially those without clothes, really are half guy, half something else. My own body does this too: from the waist up, with or without clothes, I display a White male chest. Naked, from the waist down, my body reads closest conventionally female body even though that is not how it reads to me. Clothed, from the waist down, my body is overdetermined by signifiers of whiteness and masculinity and I am just a guy. Given that the surgical production of a penis leaves much to be desired—and the penis they can build costs so much that it is out of reach for most guys—trans men cannot leave the "trans" behind and be "men." Self-naming and, by implication, self-definition, then, these crucial axioms that feminist movements fought long and hard for become tricky: I find myself at an even greater loss when it comes to finding a language to describe myself. Just recently, I have settled upon the following paradox: "I am a guy who is half lesbian." I have a long lesbian history, which I do not deny despite tremendous pressure, but have just recently come out as a straight (albeit trans-sexual) man or "I am a lesbian man." Identifying myself through paradox as a "guy who is half lesbian" really comes closest to bringing a number of historical moments together to form *something like an identity*.

Refracting identity through simile ("something like" or "closest to") is crucial to my sense of self. While I am suggesting *something like*—that is, something comparable or similar to—I am also suggesting but *something that fails to*—that is, something that fails to cohere as a thing unto itself, hence the need for the comparison to begin with. In the case of my own sense of self, for instance, the tension between "guy" and "lesbian" does the work of articulating in language what my body is currently doing through gender signifiers. The result, of course, is that many FtMs cannot always be read as "men" (without the quotation marks) in every circumstance, presuming, of course, that any man can. Take gym locker rooms as an example. These are sites of poignant contradiction within our current capitalist discourses about bodies. Gyms and health clubs are strange sites of Marxist alienation and disembodiment even in the face of an apparent hyper-embodiedness. Fragmenting bodies into "legs," "abs," "chest," "shoulders," and "arms" (and then systems like "cardio"), the class culture of working out before or after work (not employment/work as physically demanding) requires one to become, quite literally, subject to or to step into a machine that has been designed to isolate a muscle or set of muscles and work them with the goal of having them look like they do more than get worked on at the gym. The gym body is developed not necessarily from use but from an extreme form of docility, repetition, and discipline. Capitalism requires each of these when manufacturing labouring bodies. Don't get me wrong: working out is not necessarily a terrible thing to do. After years of disembodiment, I decided to take the plunge and sign up with a fitness program. Like most gyms, it relies heavily on a gendered division of space determined by conventional understandings of the supposed self-evidence of the body. Given that I read completely as male, showering in public would compromise that reading. Being undressed in a locker room—and given the degree to which straight men furtively but quite decidedly look at each other—would, quite literally, be my undoing.

Then again, signifying as a guy, which I do more consistently now that I no longer have breasts, I do so with a success that makes me politically suspect to some lesbians while at other times interesting to gay men. Toronto's Pride 2003 was an interesting experience; two things happened that marked a shift in my identity from very masculine lesbian to guy. First, I seemed to be much more interesting to gay men as an object of desire. This is evident by the way in which I am now just more noticeable; gay men flirt with me now in a way they've not done so before. At dinner, in a queer-esque restaurant, a number of men stopped by our table to say hello, pass on a pride greeting or, in one case, to invite me upstairs to an event that was happening later that night. But let me describe myself to you: in my life as a "woman," I failed miserably. I signified as extremely butch, stone butch, macho even. I am heavy-set, continue to wear a kind of crew cut, dress in black pants and crisp shirts, and do not communicate signals that could be easily construed as gay (read: gay man) in any way at all. And yet precisely because of my gender performance (if categories are necessary, I could be considered a smallish bear), I am cruised on a regular basis by gay men.

But masculinity is not the only subject of unmaking found in No Man's Land. The other thing I felt quite compelled to do during the weekend's activities was to insist that my very out lesbian-femme girlfriend of African descent hold my hand as much as possible.[7] This irony resonates even more strongly for several reasons. In a historical moment where femmes are accused of not being lesbian enough, or where queer femininity is cast in a suspicious light, it was a bit of an oddity to realize that I passed as *less than bio-guy* when outed as *something else* through my lesbian partner. Queer femininity or, as Anna Camilleri calls it, femininity gone wrong, is equally bound by contradiction, paradox, and, in the best sense of the term, perversion. The curious difference, though, where trans-folks often need to be recognized for their gender resignifications, queer femmes often rearticulate sexual scripts and do not receive enough credit for that very political work. That is, to be very specific, as a trans guy it is extremely important to me to be seen as male whereas for my femme partner, it's far more important for her to be seen as lesbian. My partner is a woman of African descent, which means that, because of our impoverished and anti-intersectional economies, a battle of dualities plays out on her body to claim her—through identification or dis-identification—either as "Black" or "queer" (but rarely both) in No Man's Land. This is not her battle but a battle over how her body is being read. The signifiers most easily read as femme and/or lesbian in our culture are those of White femininity. Lesbians of colour, including many femmes and butches, have written extensively about the whiteness of gay, lesbian, bisexual, and trans language, signifiers, histories, and so on. The semiotic deficiencies of subjectivity within White supremacy disallow signifying as Black and femme simultaneously. For my partner, visibility is frequently conditional: either she is read as her sexuality or she is read as her race. Being a racialized, gendered, and sexualized subject all at the same time is seen as unthinkable within our current paradigms of identity, which privilege—indeed, demand—singularity of identification. Models of intersectionality, which allow me, for instance, to read myself as raced (White, British), gendered (masculine), and sexualized (hetero-gendered and queerly straight) all at the same time are still sadly missing in our political lexicons. If FtMs wear masculinity as what Jay Prosser calls a second skin in order to feel visible and, strangely, invisible at the same time, femmes, on the other hand, wear a queer gendered-ness as a second skin that renders them invisible as lesbians. Femmes of colour, to risk an awkward phrase, are hailed as racialized subjects, which can render them invisible as queers *inside* queer communities. Each of these are accomplished through a triangulation, each through the other, and tell us that despite the work we have done, we have still so much more to do.

One of the most significant things I have done to unmake this supposedly femininely signified body is to have top surgery to remove my breasts. On June 9, 2003, I underwent top surgery, a euphemism for a surgical procedure properly known as bilateral mastectomy with male chest reconstruction. As I sat at my desk several days after the procedure, I wore a wide binder around my now scrawny-looking white chest. Underneath that binder, strangely similar to one I had worn when I wanted to bind my breasts, are two lateral scars where those breasts used to sit. Just above those scars are my nipples, grafted onto my newly configured chest but still healing under dressings to ensure that the grafts take. To be clear, in this procedure, the graft (the nipples) are removed completely from the skin. Once the breast tissue is removed, the nipples are then reattached as grafts. After about two weeks, the "new" nipples have attached again to the skin, only this time in a new position on the newly configured chest. But the *metaphor* of grafting is an interesting one and all too relevant to what I have just come through in this "transition."

I prefer the trope of "grafting" to "transition" because it allows me to reconfigure what I mean by trans-gender or trans-sexual. All too often, the relation between the "trans" and either "gender" or "sexual" is misread to mean that one transcends the other or that trans people, in essence, are surgically and hormonally given "new" bodies. That is, the terms "trans-gender" or "trans-sexual" are often misread to suggest a radical departure from birth bodies into squeaky clean new ones. But the terms are often misread as transcending the gender of those birth bodies into an entirely new gender. I counter that belief in my earlier book *Masculinities without Men?* but also now on and through my body; indeed, even more so now since my nipples were literally grafted back onto my chest: neither of these misreadings are as helpful as they could be.[8] My *gender* now looks different from the one I grew up with but my body is, paradoxically, almost still the same. I have the same scars, the same stretch marks, the same bumps, bruises, and birthmarks that I have always had, only it is all different now. Grafting allows me to think that relation. Not only does this trope allow me to look at the way my "new" body is grafted out of, onto, through my "old," but it is also a way of rethinking trans-gendered (read: differently gendered) bodies as effects of the sex/gender system in crisis and transition. It means my newish-looking gender is the effect of a productive failure of that manufacturing system, not its success. In those failings, trans men can become "men" in some contexts; some, but not all. But neither do trans-sexual and trans-gender folks transcend the sex/gender system; instead, trans-folks are an important site where its inabilities, as Judith Butler argues, to live up to its own imperatives (that gender be the artifact of sex) are rendered obvious.

The process of grafting, as self-remaking and queer reproduction outside of a heteronormative model, spawns (certainly for FtMs) something else outside of our sexual vocabularies and grammars. But this is not androgyny, a mix, or blending of both (read: natural) genders. As Doan (1994: 153) puts it, "the notion of hybridity resonates with doing violence to nature, which results […] in the scientific equivalent of freaks, mongrels, half-breeds and cross-breeds." This is a strategy of naturally denaturalizing biological essentialisms with a "sexual politics of heterogeneity and a vision of hybridized gender constructions outside an either/or proposition" in order to naturalize "cultural oddities, monstrosities, abnormalities, and [what appear to be] conformities" (Doan 1994: 154). The trope of grafting thus allows me to articulate the paradox signalled by "I am a lesbian man" or "I am a guy who is half lesbian." This picture of transed bodies as grafted, where one materialization is haunted by the other, as opposed to crossing or exiting, also allows me to articulate the radical dependencies that these identities (lesbian and trans guy or, to update the lexicon, female masculinity and trans-sexual masculinity) have for me but also with each other historically (the invert + the lesbian + the trans-sexual). To say "I am a lesbian man" or "I am a guy who is half lesbian" both materializes or externalizes a body that is not always immediately visible yet is still absolutely necessary for the performative paradox to work. It means to answer "yes" to "Am I that name?"[9] and to amend the question so that it reads multiply instead of singularly: "Am I this and that at the same time?" Thus, intelligibility for the female-to-male trans-sexual man means contesting the alignment of bodies, genders, and sexualities to force a crisis by grafting articulations onto each other in the same way that my nipple grafts work. I remember the day I heard a trans man say about his former breasts: "It's such a paradox to have to cut some part of myself off in order to feel whole." Those words are inscribed painfully across my chest today more than ever, but make no mistake: this is the body not as foundation but as archive; this is the same chest, the same body, the same flesh I have always known, only now its text is totally different.[10]

For all my bravado around top surgery, one of the things I have learned through the process is that these are costly choices. Certainly they are costly financially and now that many provincial governments have de-listed these services, trans-folks are left to their own devices to pay for vital procedures. In addition, there's something about going to my extremely trans-friendly doctor that I find profoundly disturbing. My anxiety traces a particular distress around the medically overdetermined conditions of embodiment. This is still the medicalization of bodies, genders, and lives, and as much as the diagnosis "gender identity disorder" is a formal alibi, it still reflects the reality that trans-folks are forced to make the best choices for ourselves in a field of overdetermined possibilities. Even though Toronto's Clark Institute is no longer the sole gatekeeper of sex-reassignment procedures, the job of dispensing hormone therapies and giving referrals to surgeons, etc., still rests with usually non-transed physicians. And the means of rendering oneself intelligible, which is especially true for FtMs who do not achieve full embodiment of their chosen gender, is still the clinical alibi of "gender identity disorder."

That said, politically, the pressure to complete paperwork to change my former F to an M is tremendous. While I signify a version of White masculinity,

I have chosen to keep the F. The existence of that F, though, has led me to draw some rather interesting conclusions about its limits. When I have handed that document over to various individuals, most people seem to pay little attention, if any, to the F. I am often, because of my gender presentation, dis-identified with that F. Similarly, my image of myself as masculine is becoming reoriented in the process as well. Such incommensurability between self and body is the No Man's Land in which transed lives are lived. While medicalized interventions render this gap less dangerous, they do not, at least for FtMs, render the gap non-existent. Since my surgery, I am aware that I signify quite differently and that I need to transform my own consciousness to keep up. I now find myself asking what kind of *guy* am I presenting because masculinity on the perception of a male body is quite different than masculinity on the perception of a female body. But I am still a guy with an F designation. This discursive contradiction, paradox even, allows me, as Duggan and McHugh suggest (1996: 110) in the "Fem(me)inist Manifesto," to "inhabit normal abnormally." It means, as the best feminist interventions have always told us, that I need to be painfully aware of how I signify, of what kinds of power accrue to my whiteness and masculinity, and then work against both of those to challenge those power grids. It means, as a White man, outing myself whenever and wherever possible as a race traitor, not because I am partnered with a woman of colour but because of my commitment to an anti-racist critical practice that includes doing the pedagogical work of challenging racism among other straight White men. Who better to occupy the space of *guy* but former lesbians who have walked the streets as women, loved as fierce and sometimes stone butches, and who have come of political age in the context of lesbian-feminism? For me, that's a proud history that does not get left behind in the operating room.

But it is precisely *because* of that same gender performance that some lesbians, on the other hand, have expressed frustration when I, a straight White man, appear in lesbian (although not lesbian/woman only) spaces. The most pernicious of these chills occurred at United Kingdom 2: International Drag King Show, a trans-friendly and literate event produced in Toronto that showcases drag king performances from across North America and, this year, Amsterdam. The irony resonates strongly: at an event that offers female and trans masculinity for consumption, I passed so well as a non-transed person—indeed, as just a straight White guy—that my presence was troubling to one young woman in particular who felt little discomfort about communicating her disapproval. That chill was repeated a number of other times during Toronto's Dyke March day (I did not go on the dyke march) so that I quite aggressively hunted down a t-shirt that would, at the very least, dis-identify my seemingly heterosexual masculinity with heteronormativity.

That said, then, if it is possible to render my masculinity anti-heteronormative, then might it also be possible to remake whiteness, not necessarily just self-conscious but similarly incoherent? That is, if I've been suggesting that trans men risk incoherence, can White masculinity also risk incoherence as a political strategy, one that refuses the hegemonic bargains offered to White trans manhood? White masculinity is, of course, an intersection of parts where a fantasy of singularity is privileged instead. As I have indicated earlier in conversation with James Baldwin, whiteness, in other words, is secured by its violent imperative of universal, categorical singularity (that is, non-intersectionality). Trans manhood has the ability to exist on a similar frequency as biological masculinity without the coherence or clarity of meaning. Trans White masculinity is key for its failure to cohere, as I indicated at the end of Chapter 1, into hegemonic or visible *matter*. (Again, simile is key here.) Dionne Brand presents a similar argument about this in her work, *A Map to the Door of No Return*, when she writes of bodies as matter being socially constructed with extremely potent stakes:

> There are ways of constructing the world—that is, of putting it together each morning, what it should look like piece by piece—and I don't feel that I share that with the people of this small town. Each morning I think we wake up and open our eyes and set the particles of forms together—we make solidity with our eyes and with the matter in our brains. [...] We collect each molecule, summing them up into "flesh" or "leaf" or "water" or "air." Before that everything is liquid, ubiquitous and mute. We accumulate information over our lives which brings various things into solidity, into view. What I am afraid of is that waking up in another room, minutes away by car, the mechanic wakes up and takes my face for a target [...] He cannot see me when I come into the gas station; he sees something else [...] as if I do not exist [...] or as if something he cannot understand has arrived—as if something he despises has arrived. A thing he does not recognize. Some days when I go to the gas station [...] I drive through the possibility of losing solidity at any moment. (Brand 2002: 141–142)

Brand argues for race what Fausto-Sterling and Butler argue about sex and gender and what I want to advocate as a trans practice of masculinity:

> To be material is to speak about the process of materialization. And if viewpoints about [identity] are already embedded in our philosophical

concepts of how matter forms into bodies, the matter of bodies cannot form a neutral, pre-existing ground from which to understand the origin of [...] different. Since matter already contains notions of [identity], it cannot be a neutral recourse on which to build "scientific" or "objective" theories of [the trans subject] ... the idea of the material comes to us already tainted, containing within it pre-existing ideas about [identity] ... the body as a system [...] simultaneously produces and is produced by social meanings. (Fausto-Sterling 2000: 22–23)

Entrance into these fictionalities of matter, of coherent White skin, is purchased through an ideological belief in a naturalized whiteness and naturalized masculinity. The reading of a body as gendered male and racialized White involves presenting signifiers within an economy where the signifiers accumulate toward the appearance of a coherently gendered and racialized body.

Baldwin's work on the price of the White ticket is crucial here. "White people are not white," writes James Baldwin (1985: xiv), "part of the price of the white ticket is to delude themselves into believing that they are." Baldwin echoes sentiments of thinker W.E.B. Du Bois, who argued that there is no such thing as pure categorical whiteness. The existence of the White race produces the unconscious (at best) willingness of those assigned to it to place their racial interests above class or any other interests they hold. Whiteness, in other words, is bound by and is, in effect, secured by its imperative of universal singularity. Entrance into the fictionality of whiteness is purchased through an ideological class belief in naturalized whiteness. What White is, then, is a class-based race: the higher up you go, the whiter you get. One is not born White, one buys his or her way into whiteness and *becomes* White. That price, Baldwin writes, includes, necessitates even, believing in the fiction of whiteness as signifier of the universal subject, the just plain, simple, and singular Man and Woman. But the price is afforded by what later theorists of whiteness will call its psychological and social wages: skin colour and class (upward) mobility. This is what the men and women of my ancestry purchased for me off the labour of their class-based whiteness (what I previously called off-White, White, but not middle-class White): entrance, as an educated adult, into a whitened middle class. While I grew up on welfare, we became *whiter* through the generations.

While I am no longer working class (the transition into that whitened middle class was a far harder transition for me than "changing" genders), I continue to be very aware of a rising discourse of whiteness, which, as some writers detail, is racializing class-based whiteness in what seem to me to be all the wrong ways. Five years ago I would have argued that self-consciousness for White people could be anything but wrong. But as many race theorists have taught us, White supremacy, like other colonial systems, is historical and amenable to new circumstances and critique. In the last few decades, there has been a huge proliferation of thinking and writing about whiteness. The emerging field of critical whiteness scholarship has an interdisciplinary past, influenced by work being done in two fields simultaneously: on the one hand, the work of American historiographers have produced very interesting articulated histories of class and race. Historian David Roediger's books: *Towards the Abolition of Whiteness* and *The Wages of Whiteness* both explore the emergence of whiteness as a labour force in the post-slavery U.S. Theodore Allen's book, *The Invention of the White Race* similarly traces the way that Irish immigrants, like those portrayed in *Gangs of New York*, settled in the U.S. and *became* White. While the work of historians has provided critical accounts of the moments when White identities first began to do particular types of work in North America, the work of novelists and literary critics or cultural theorists began to theorize the impact of representational and canon-formation practices that construct their canons and readers as White. I will mention two cultural theorists whose work has been most important for me.

The first cultural theorist whose work is seminal to whiteness scholarship is film critic Richard Dyer. In 1988, he published an extremely important essay simply called "White." In that early essay (subsequently published later as part of a full-length book of the same name), Dyer enacts a theoretical shift that enables us to ask the questions about whiteness that we are asking today. This shift shares much in common with the contradictions about sexuality detailed by Eve Sedgwick in *Epistemology of the Closet* (1990). Questions about race and sexuality have been bound by a set of epistemological contradictions: on the one hand, some questions of identity race theory have been conservatively constructed as what Sedgwick calls a *minoritizing* discourse (seeing that identity as an issue of active importance only for a small, distinct, relatively fixed group, like Caribbean-Canadians or First Nations peoples, for instance). On the other hand, what we need to do instead is to retheorize race and sexuality as what Sedgwick dubs a "universalizing discourse," an issue or discourse of active importance in the lives of subjects across the spectrum of identity categories. This particular shift in thinking allows us, like Dyer and Sedgwick in their work, to ask particular kinds of questions about whiteness and heterosexuality, questions that shift the critical gaze from the so-called racialized object (Black people, etc.) to the so-called racial subject (White folks doing the looking). In other words, instead of allowing the White critical gaze to look and taxonomize colours or cultures, a universalizing discourse allows us to turn the gaze back onto whiteness. And shifting that gaze is exactly what Dyer's essay accomplishes. Where race theory interrogates the production of racialized identities, critical whiteness studies examines the ways that whiteness *qua* whiteness has somehow been left out of those terms.

The effect of turning that gaze back on itself is a fascinating one. According to the ideologies of White supremacy within which we all live, racist constructions of race function best by allowing whiteness to remain unmarked as a race. One of the consequences of allowing whiteness to remain unmarked as a race, as Dyer suggests, is that whiteness becomes the norm. Whiteness, in other words, constructs itself as coterminous with the endless plenitude of human diversity, with the non-particularizable general. As Dyer (1988: 45–46) notes,

> On the one hand [...] white domination is reproduced by the way that white people colonize the definition of the normal. [...] on the other hand, if the invisibility of whiteness colonizes the definition of other norms—class, gender, heterosexuality, nationality and so on—it also masks whiteness as itself a category. [...] This property of whiteness, to be everything and nothing, is the source of its representational power.

What this means is that whiteness remains so entirely hyper-visible as everything that it also becomes, paradoxically, invisible as nothing, the norm, as an invisible backdrop against which all other races are produced. It also means that whiteness was not a found category but one that was historically invented and/or constructed.

This construction of whiteness as the norm or as the absence of race or colour is curious. As Dyer notes, where whiteness imagines itself as a pure, non-mixed, absence of race or colour, it represents a curious scientific paradox. That is, scientifically speaking, on the colour spectrum, blackness is actually the absence of colour, not whiteness. How is it, then, that in the categorization of racial subjects that whiteness represents absence of colour, and blackness is overdetermined as, metaphorically speaking, all colours or just as colour itself? Black is always marked as a colour and is always particularized whereas White is not really anything, not an identity, not a particularizing quality because it is, supposedly, everything. And how is it possible that representations of whiteness always show it as a bound category, as an identity that is absolute, bound, and supposedly impermeable and utterly unconscious of itself as a race?

Toni Morrison's 1992 book *Playing in the Dark: Whiteness and the Literary Imagination* similarly argues for the necessity of reorienting that taxonomizing White gaze back on itself. As an American novelist, Morrison has been writing about race and American history for quite some time in both her fiction and literary criticism, the most important of which foreground the representational and ideological relations between whiteness and blackness in American literature. Morrison asks hard questions in her book, such as what difference has it made to American literature that its imagined readership has been assumed to be White? A great deal of work has addressed the "Black image" in American literature; what about the White image? "My project," Morrison argues, "is an effort to avert the critical gaze from the so-called object to the subject; from the described and imagined to the describers and imaginers; from the serving to the served" (90). This critical move established the field of whiteness studies around the question of why White is the default setting of so much discourse about race. Morrison and Dyer echo each other in their arguments: There is, in effect, a quality of transparency to whiteness as if being White means lacking a racial identity, a quality that is, according to the historians, completely a product of history. The outcome, according to Morrison, is an American paradox where the ideal of freedom is historically rooted in the institution of slavery, an imbrication or connection that America and, by implication, American ideologies and canonical literatures, can never separate.

The historians support Morrison's argument. What Roediger, Morgan, Allen, and others found in 19th-century American history is strangely similar to what is articulated in the films *Bulworth* or *White Boyz* or even the film I will turn my attention to in a moment, Eminem's *8 Mile*, and that is this: the historians of race have uncovered a long historical relation between race and class that suggests, in a nutshell, that in post-reconstruction America—that is, after the Civil War and the so-called end of slavery—poor White labourers who were loyal to the southern economic system that slavery built received, like newly freed Black labourers, a low wage, but were also additionally compensated in part by a sort of public and psychological wage: deference, better schools, access to public facilities, etc. That means, in other words, that poor White workers were offered the possibility of upward mobility because of their race, which Black labourers could rarely achieve. But who were these White labourers? The historians tell us that these poor White labourers were often wave after wave of white-skinned immigrant groups emigrating to the "promised land." As they did, the racial economy of the U.S. allowed despised ethnic groups, especially those with whiter skin, to transcend their minority status and, once they acquired *the price of the ticket*, join the great imaginary *whitened* American majority (hence, the birth of the fiction of the melting pot). The existence of the White race depends on the willingness of those assigned to it to place their racial interests above class or any other interests they hold. Whiteness, in other words, is bound by and is, in effect, a part of the very thing it claims not to be: *of colour.* Entrance into the fictionality of whiteness is purchased through an ideological class belief, which asserts that a pure whiteness exists.

Into this fray, in 1993, enters feminist theorist Ruth Frankenberg and her book *White Women, Race Matters: The Social Construction of Whiteness.* Frankenberg is clearly influenced by the work of Morrison and Dyer, as well as the other theorists, but her work takes the paradigms mapped earlier and shapes them around the breakdown of the feminist cultural consensus around race. What was it, she asks, about the work that White feminists in particular were doing or not doing that contributed to that breakdown? Or, as Frankenberg (1993: 8) puts it so succinctly,

> it became clear in the context of a critique of white feminist racism, there are multiple problems in attempting to use white women's lives as a resource for analyzing gender domination in its entirety. Through the 80s and into the present, work predominantly by women of color has been transforming feminist analysis, drawing attention to the white-centredness, and more generally, the false universalizing claims.

She continues: "Women of color were the first to advance frameworks for understanding the intersection in women's lives of gender, race, sexuality, race and class" (Frankenberg 1993: 8). The implication here is that social construction of these identities not only produces *what we see,* but, more significantly if we are White, *what we can't see.* And what whiteness cannot see is crucial.

Frankenberg's argument is brilliantly simple, and I want to sum it up in the following points (some of this will sound familiar already from Dyer and Morrison). She argues that we are all, regardless of skin colour, living racially shaped lives, although we live them within a system of unequal impact. That is, to have White privilege is to have structural advantage or race privilege, but to be White does not mean to be without a discernible race. She also raises the question of exactly what we mean by the term "whiteness." Is it a set of physical traits (pale skin)? A set of behavioural characteristics (playing hockey) or ways of acting? A nationality? A bureaucratic category (like on a census form)? She answers that whiteness is all of these and so much more. Race, like gender, is not a constructed and deployed scientific fact but a constructed and deployed cultural fact whose meanings are written onto bodies.

Whiteness is, according to Frankenberg, invisible and unmarked as a racial category but hyper-visible so as to appear natural and normative. The White subject is therefore unknowing and unseeing and the subjects of colour know more about White subjects than the White subjects themselves. Whiteness is empty, having little content that is constituted by appropriation. It is, in other words, understood as a lack of cultural distinctiveness and authenticity. Whiteness is structural privilege. But she also suggests that whiteness is socially constructed and signifies multiple things all at the same time, the least of which are the social and cultural mechanisms that produce it. Some examples of those social and cultural mechanisms are evident through a further elaboration of an intersectional model that can be unpacked further around what "whiteness" means: whiteness refers simultaneously to social locations, discourses, and material relations all at the same time, but whiteness also changes over time and space and is in no way a trans-historical essence; whiteness is also a complex constructed product of local, regional, national, and global relations, past and present that are linked to relations of domination. Naming that whiteness, then, she argues, has the potential to displace it from the unmarked, unnamed status that is itself an effect of its dominance. And, finally and most importantly, it is co-constructed with an intersectional range of other axes of identity (gender, sexuality, class, nation, and so on), but this co-construction is asymmetrical because the term "whiteness" signals the production and reproduction of dominance, normativity, and privilege.

Again, by implication, there is also a link between where one stands and what one perceives. The larger implication of this, she suggests, is that the "oppressed" can see with the greatest clarity not only their own position but also that of the oppressor/privileged and indeed the shape of the social system as a whole: "to speak of whiteness is to assign everyone a place in the relations of racism" (6). Naming whiteness exposes its fundamental work. It also corrects the lacunae in perception; especially around the question of how is it that white folks do not see their racialness and how that is a uniquely defining and structural feature of whiteness. Finally, because we are talking about all of the things that whiteness references (that is, because it is a social construction with profound social and real political effects), meaning systems are not controllable necessarily by individual intentions, especially when those intentions actualize in a social economy grounded in differential impact.

What's at stake in this particular set of arguments is a denaturalization of whiteness. That is, denaturalizing whiteness means to universalize whiteness, not as the norm but as just another race among a spectrum of racial identities that could do the work of articulating both whiteness and anti-racism work differently, albeit another race with systemic power. As I began to research some of the books I have mentioned, which are only just the tip of the iceberg, I realized that whiteness, like many of the things I have been exploring in this work, has a history and representational currency. Thinking through representations of whiteness in popular culture and fiction allows me to argue not just the persistence of racism around us but also the ways in which identities can either challenge or be complicit with that persistence. If, as the historians suggest, race and class, that is, blackness and working-class whiteness are conceptual cousins, then the film *8 Mile*, is, we could suggest, a text that wants to stage the slippage of boundaries between categories. That said, this slippage between categories, especially as it is depicted by White filmmakers, is, as I will argue through *8 Mile*, a reconsolidation of the supremacy of whiteness rather than its deconstruction. This reconsolidation is one form of coherence I want to work my body against.

Whiteness will always force its subjects to privilege their own unmarked invisibilities over any other marker of "difference" among its subjects (class, gender, and sexuality). But the price of becoming White is quite different than the price and, or, more accurately, the cost of knowing one is White. These two things are not exactly the same thing at all; *becoming* White means that one is no longer aware of oneself as a race and believes that one simply melts into the amorphous mass of the norm; *knowing* one is White means understanding oneself as a product of White supremacy or systemic racism that is larger than one individual and that also precedes our entry into the public domain. How can whiteness be used to dismantle that larger system? And, more importantly, is that what we see the character of Rabbit (Eminem) doing in *8 Mile*? I will answer, with help from an extremely important theorist, Annalee Newitz, in the negative. A film like this appropriates the practice of naming whiteness not as a tool of dismantling White supremacy, but of dismantling challenges to it instead.

Firstly, *8 Mile* is a thinly disguised autobiography of the performer Eminem. Where *Fight Club* shows us the dangers of the types of White middle-class masculinities created in capitalism through this splitting of self between idealization and actual, *8 Mile* functions as an example of White hegemonic thinking by infusing ideas about whiteness and class into our thinking about gender. Most importantly, though, this film depict the limits of our ways of thinking about cultural work. We often believe that those with talent will somehow be discovered (*American Idol*) and then move into the public realm. *8 Mile* shows us that even access to the entry points of popular culture requires cultural and financial resources: for both the male and female working-class young people, Rabbit and Alex, this means money to produce a demo tape and/or a portfolio that will allow them to transcend their working-class environment. We can extrapolate from this exactly what many cultural theorists have been telling us for quite some time now: culture emerges directly from the material conditions of life; the only caveat is whether we know that or not.

Secondly, though, and I think this is far more controversial, *8 Mile* attempts to argue that given this truism, rap music and hip hop cultures not only reflect the racialized conditions of social realities (the fact that we still live in a White supremacy), but make a powerful connection between those racial conditions, gender, and class. The film stages a series of anxieties about whiteness and voice. In the film's first opening mirror scene, Rabbit is not speaking; this silence is followed by his inarticulateness on stage. What's he doing at that mirror? We see him silently going through the motions, demonstrating something similar to what drag kings do, which is to imitate the choreography of a musical form and, by doing so, construct its message. But we also see Rabbit looking into that mirror, asking a question similar to one I have reiterated here: Am I that, perhaps not name, but image? As Newitz and Dyer suggest to us, whiteness is a socially manufactured fiction shaped by systems of race, although not necessarily in the same way that people of colour are. If this is true, then White supremacy economies organize themselves around the hyper-visibility of people of colour as "different," and invisibility of whiteness as just somehow the norm. Whiteness is conceived of as the dominant or hegemonic norm; it is an unmarked, unnamed system of meanings that also conditions what one can see based on where one is looking from. If Frankenberg is right—that there is a link between where one stands and what one perceives—then Rabbit goes through the motions of a cultural form on which, according to the ideologies of the film, he has no "authentic" claim by virtue of his whiteness. The genre is a performative, then, and the answer he hears in that scene is "No."

If this is true, then the entire film from this point on is about Rabbit attempting to authenticate his use, as a White performer, of that musical and aesthetic form. The first time we hear Rabbit's music is on the bus. It is ironic that he, as a White man, is sitting at the back of the bus, which is not an insignificant seating arrangement where, by association, Rabbit is blackened. The bus's route through a very specific sense of place—through the remains of a city—is significant as we also see the music forming organically from Rabbit's relationship to these images of a ruined city. His hands begin moving to the sound of his own music in the voice-over. That location may not be Black for Rabbit, but it is certainly poor and this is what lends him credibility.

But the film, like many working-class transcendent films, is also interested in asking questions about the possibilities of transcending these gender, racial, and economic conditions. Both Rabbit and Alex are trying to get out of the conditions that produced them. But gender modulates the possibilities of transcending class. How? First, through sex, where we see sex, especially the scene between Rabbit and Alex in the factory, as quite literally a function of capitalism and the machine. If that is true, and we see Alex trading on her body with Wink to attempt to get out, then the film begins to develop its second narrative crisis: what will Rabbit need to trade to produce his demo to get out? That free demo that Rabbit is trying to make requires getting "free" studio time. What is the cost of that "free" time? It is Rabbit committing himself to a contract with Wink that is, in essence, not different from Alex's. This relation or sense of "selling out" is sexualized and queered; it is emphasized in the next scene where we see Rabbit performing at the lunch truck when his competitor makes fun of a gay man named Paul. How Rabbit responds to this is telling: "Paul's gay," Rabbit says to his competitor. "You're the faggot" because he has sold out. There is a link for masculinity in this film, then, where selling out is the mark of the "faggot." This is the personal crisis for Rabbit: will he or won't he sell out? There is a strange tension here between who sells what in order to get out. Future (Mekhi Phifer's character) sums this up: "Free means a dick up your ass." Given that the group of artists who control the recording studio are Black while those who control the "Black" streets are called, with a vicious racist irony, "Leaders of the Free World," for poor White men in this context, transcending the material conditions of poverty is likened to passivity and effeminacy where the colour of that dick is Black and the ass is White.

But there is also a curious tension around the possibility of language as a site of ideological conflict and power. If being silent and doing your job ("selling out") is what it takes to survive capitalism as a worker, then using language in meaningful ways in culturally specific representations (i.e., music) is tremendously important to say what cannot be said as a worker: there is in the film a difference between "talking shit and living at home with our mammas" and coming into language through music and culture. One is doing nothing; the other is fighting and resisting with words. This is why that opening mirror scene is crucial; it shows Rabbit beginning to find voice, but it also shows us masculinity as a prosthetic process, as a guise, something put on. This trajectory into voice is the real narrative crisis in the film. Where do we see Rabbit speaking? (1) at work on car singing about being trailer trash; (2) on the street after work before the rap group, Leaders of the Free World, shows up; (3) around the lunch truck; (4) in the trailer with his sister; (5) in the battles at the shelter. Not until Rabbit can articulate himself as White can he come into voice, although how that occurs is very telling about the anxieties of whiteness. He, in essence, steals words, names himself White, and silences his opponent.

Even though, on a surface level, both Eminem as a cultural figure and the film itself might be drawing our attention to class as an important feature in the work hip hop cultures perform, as well as the argument that the material conditions of life directly affect cultural production, the film positions whiteness as vulnerable, oppressed, and heroic in its battle against the forces of tyranny—forces racialized as Black—which is a very odd way of thinking about race in the 21st century. Given these complex racializations, *8 Mile* is a perfect example of a very sneaky and popular racist backlash against necessary encroachments onto whiteness. This backlash is detailed by Annalee Newitz (1997) in her essay, "White Savagery and Humiliation, or a New Racial Consciousness in the Media." Newitz is critical of how whiteness is identifying itself in popular culture. She asks two extremely important questions that I think are vital to an unpacking of these articulations and discontents of whiteness *after* the emergence of the whiteness field as mapped by Dyer and Morrison: (1) How do independent music and film reflect how White people think people of colour view them? and (2) How does that triangulation of a self-image through a fantasy of how whiteness is perceived by people of colour construct how White people see themselves? Her work is premised upon Frankenberg's assertion that standpoint determines what one can see, suggesting that people of colour know far more about White people than White people know about themselves. And with this, she folds her second question into her first, arguing that "It would seem that whiteness only becomes visible to itself when whites discover their racial particularity in the imaginations of racial others" (Frankenberg 1993: 132).

Newitz also argues that there are some forms of whiteness that have had a particular kind of visibility. In her thesis, she argues further that one way we might understand White racial identity at the close of the 20th century is as a social construction characterized most forcefully by a growing awareness of its own internal contradictions and a growing deployment of class divisions within whiteness. These are manifested in White-on-White class conflicts that produce a White racial self-consciousness based on various forms of divisiveness and self-loathing. White consciousness, she argues, emerges as a distinct and visible racial identity when it can be identified as class or as primitive, inhuman, and, ironically, hyper-visible: poor White trash. She continues to suggest that lower-class whiteness functions as a racially marked identity (Newitz 1997: 138). Whites who are not "trash" seem innocent of racially marked whiteness. Poor Whites are, in other words, less White and guilty of a "savagery" that upper-class Whites have transcended.

At the same time this particular deflection and deferral can be converted into what Newitz calls a confession of whiteness or a racialized look or positioning of redemption, a gesture of concern that will give us the appearance of innocence or redemption as White but which takes the place of real action to eliminate social injustice (Newitz 1997: 139). It becomes, in other words, a form of self-punishment that gets played out within and among White groups, producing a White nihilism. Nihilism was a doctrine that denied purpose, hope, a larger order, and that translated quickly into the self-destructive behaviours we've seen before. In a racial context, it is the actualization of what she argues is at the core of White supremacy to begin with: fear, inferiority, and failure. "When whites," she argues, "are put in touch with that fear, a kind of self-destructive nihilism results" (Newitz 1997: 139). This then converts into a pre-emptive self-hatred. Whites, in her estimation, imagine themselves as people of colour might and then name themselves pre-emptively to circumvent the power of being named by others. "One might understand these narratives," she argues, "as fantasies about whites resolving their racial problems without ever having to deal with people of colour" (Newitz 1997: 139). This is, in other words, a form of psychological defence, one that is racist and "a politically reactionary form of ideological defense" (Newitz 1997: 144). No one, after all, can insult you if you insult yourself first.

This is precisely the kind of strategy that Rabbit takes at the end of the film to win the battle. Whiteness takes its content, as Newitz suggests, from its relations with others. Naming oneself as White trash is precisely how Rabbit wins the contest. The fantasy of whiteness is that somehow it has shape only when it imagines itself being identified through the language and naming practices of people of colour. But is not this still a kind of appropriation of voice? Part of what I am asking about this film, and indeed about Eminem's popularity among young, White working-class youth, is whether or not it is functioning as a text that dismantles whiteness in a politically useful way or if it is a film that simply inverts positions to suggest that it is, in the context of the film, Black culture discriminating against poor whiteness. Is it really counter-cultural to suggest, as the film does, that women and, in this case, Black cultures now hold so much power that they are making it impossible for White men? Or is this film part of a backlash against the advances made by these social movements? This is a remarkably "intersectional" film that works against the deconstructive labour of our frameworks. In this instance, the master's tools and labour are being used to rebuild the house.

It is increasingly seductive for FtM trans-sexual men, especially for those of us who are White, to claim a similar position. I have been suggesting all along that the labour of making oneself—indeed, of becoming a man—is fraught with responsibilities that go with the territory whether we know it or not. This labour is not unlike the labour of capitalized waged work, especially when, as the whiteness theorists have told us, whiteness accrues with it an additional social and psychological wage. The question then is less how much of ourselves do we sell with intention and more how much we are willing to articulate our bodies against the hegemonic bargain offered to us. For me, that is the measure of the privilege of masculinity without also being The Man.

I like to think that my grandmother and her co-workers understood something of these stakes as working-class and union women. If class and race are the subject of invention and ideological production, then theorizing trans-sexual issues as *labour* also does not seem that strange to me. In many ways, that's precisely the argument of this book. Gender identities—that is, gendered selves—are the product of, but also condition, particular kinds of labour. If the sex/gender system works, like any other ideological system, through misrecognition where we misperceive ourselves as natural human beings rather than as ideologically produced subjects, then it requires, as many theorists have pointed out, our complicit co-operation in order to accomplish that misrecognition. One of the rewards of that activity is the belief in a natural gender that is not man-made. Feminism has been arguing now for over a century that active insubordination with the imperatives of that system is one of the ways to make change happen and to refuse to allow that system to accomplish itself. A new century demands that feminism also begin to acknowledge its own complicity with the biological essentialisms at the core of the sex/gender systems. If it is true that gender identities are acts of co-production, then the process of becoming a self, of making a self, which is so much a part of what trans-identities tell us, is also labour that can be used against the sex/gender system. A North Carolina drag king named Pat Triarch calls gender queers and trans-folks "deconstruction workers," who, by quite literally putting misfitting bodies on the (dis-assembly) line, begin to resist and rebuild the *man-made* gender imperatives that pass as those of nature. These bodies are not bodies as foundation but trans-bodies as archive, witness, risking political incoherence.

NOTES

1. The pedantic distinction between "trans-gender" and "trans-sexual" cannot hold, especially for female-to-male trans-sexual men for whom surgeries are always incomplete. To avoid being repetitive here, I used the prefix *trans-* to signify subjectivities where bodies are at odds with gender presentation, regardless of whether that misalignment is self-evident in conventional ways or not. The entire question of what's visible, when, how, and by whom is precisely what is at stake in this chapter, so policing or prescribing or hierarchizing kinds of political embodiment is a topical identity politic and moral panic that I eschew.

2. I am not claiming to be outside of White supremacy, nor am I claiming that somehow working-class whiteness is not White. What I am trying to explore here is the possibility within intersectionality of different kinds of whiteness, positioned at different angles to power in White supremacy, where the type of power is mitigated by overlapping and intersecting vectors of power by class, able-bodied-ness, sexuality, gender, and so forth. But the relation to racialized power is constant and I am not at all suggesting otherwise.

3. There is a curious and undertheorized history of what has come to be known as the "self-help discourse"; there was a time in early second wave feminism, due to the work of rape crisis and battered women's/shelter activists/workers, when recovering from the trauma and violence of the sex/gender system was an inherently political act of resistance. Hegemonic appropriations of these ideas rearticulated this notion of a reconfigured self in extremely conservative ways: self is what cosmetic procedures provide ("The Swan"); it's the product of an upper-class leisure-time activity (in most recent years, "Oprah"); self is what's taken up by the beauty myths and also what's used as an advertising strategy (see Subway's new campaign for lighter food consumption, which shows several people stating why they prefer Subway's new light menu, including a young, blonde, White woman from the anorexia demographic saying "I choose to actually eat"); a newly configured self is what Dr. Phil's diet campaign berates and shames folks into becoming. One of the few feminist texts to begin examining this history is Ann Cvetkovich's (2003) *An Archive of Feelings: Trauma, Sexuality and Lesbian Public Cultures.*

4. This is, of course, the primary trope and political rallying cry of Leslie Feinberg's (1991) novel, *Stone Butch Blues,* one of the most important working-class and trans narratives to call for a practice of strategic unmaking.

5. The CUPE 3903 Women's Caucus has not only counted trans-sexual women amongst its members, but in a truly unprecedented intervention in this border war, recently changed its name (it is now the "Trans Identified and Women

Identified" Caucus) to create space for trans-sexual men as well. It is clear that this local is able to fold the concerns of its trans-sexual and trans-gendered members into its mandate as issues of labour, not "lifestyle" as the Ontario Conservative government has so deemed.

6. By "tribal" I refer to the tribal organization of premodern Ireland as it was depicted in the film, not the current obnoxious fashion among White folks (read: "Survivor") to imagine themselves as members of urban tribes.

7. The work of this section owes a debt to OmiSoore H. Dryden, my partner, with whom I have spent many pleasurable hours in delightful conversation.

8. *Masculinities without Men?* (2004).

9. This is an allusion to Denise Riley's (1988) extremely important work, *"Am I That Name?": Feminism and the Category of "Women" in History*.

10. See Ann Cvetkovich, *An Archive of Feelings*. On the relation between trauma and counter-cultural resistance movements as an archive or record of trauma but also of resistance, Cvetkovich (2003: 20) writes: "I am interested [...] in the way trauma digs itself in at the level of the everyday, and in the incommensurability of large-scale events and the ongoing material details of experience .... I hope to seize authority over trauma discourses from medical and scientific discourse in order to place it back in the hands of those who make culture, as well as to forge new models for how affective life can serve as the foundation for public but counter-cultural archive as well."

Chapter 5

"STRANGE SISTERS": TORONTO
FEMME FRENZIES

I conjured her, the woman in the red dress, her hair the colour of night …
I wondered what she would do in my place. She became a muse in my life,
as real as anything—an angel, a siren …
> —Anna Camilleri, *I Am a Red Dress* (2004: 115)

Seeing is the tithe, not the prize.
> —Anna Camilleri and Chloë Brushwood Rose,
> *Brazen Femme* (2002: 11)

THIS CHAPTER ON QUEER FEMININITY IS A STARK CONTRADICTION IN A
book with such a masculine title. The irony of this does not escape me. But
if I advocate risking incoherence as a political strategy in other parts of this
book, what better place to demonstrate the efficacy of that strategy than to
facilitate the rupturing of a work on masculinity by queer femininity? Stuart
Hall details the decentring significance of rupture as a political, discursive,
and texture strategy by creating what he calls conjunctures, what feminism has
been calling intersections. Arguing that such detours and ruptures "reorganize
the fields in quite concrete ways," he goes on to suggest that "again and again,
the so-called unfolding of [a field of] studies was interrupted by a break,
by real ruptures, by exterior forces; the interruption [caused by] new ideas,
which decentre what looked like accumulating practice of the work … [this
is] theoretical work as interruption" (Hall 1996: 268). These interruptions,
ruptures, and displacements ground intellectual and institutionalized academic
fields, such as the ones I am dabbling in here (masculinity studies, queer
theory, trans-sexual studies, etc.), in political actualities, keeping them from
becoming too codified.

> The question is what happens when a field, which I've been trying to describe
> in a very punctuated, dispersed and interrupted way, as constantly changing
> directions, and which is defined as a political project, tries to develop itself as
> some kind of coherent theoretical intervention? Or, to put the same question
> in reverse, what happens when an academic and theoretical enterprise tries

to […] make a difference in the institutional world in which it is located? It asks us to assume that culture will always work through its textualities— and at the same time that textuality is never enough. I want to insist that until and unless [it] learns to live with this tension, a tension that all textual practices must assume—a tension which Said describes as the study of the text in its affiliations with "institutions. Offices, agencies, classes, academies, corporations, groups, ideologically defined parties and professions, races and genders"—it will have renounced its "worldly" vocation. That is to say, unless and until one respects the necessary displacement of culture, and yet is always irritated by its failure to reconcile itself with other questions that matter […] as a project, an intervention, [it] remains incomplete …. [ruptures] constantly allow the one to irritate, bother and disturb the other, without insisting on some final theoretical closure. (Hall 1996: 271–272)

I belabour this introduction and quote Hall at length because I want to posit as a truism that masculinity studies—whether it is bio-, trans-, or female masculinities—has not yet fully earned the right to accomplish its work without constantly being reminded of the "worldly" stakes of the project. That is, while many of the key thinkers of the field of masculinity studies remain committed to a feminist and anti-racist practice, the slide into anti-feminism and racism, on occasion by trans-sexual men as well, continually haunts its practice. Failing to establish scholarly coherence, what Hall calls "final theoretical closure," is what marks masculinities studies, especially the place where whiteness studies and masculinities studies overlap, as potentially efficacious. Where that potency will go, once institutional recognition and credibility occur, remains to be seen and so needs to be continually checked by displacements back into feminism and, in this case, fem(me)inism.

Historically, femme subjectivities have almost always been subsumed by female and butch masculinity. Over 100 years of sexological research, for instance, has rarely, if ever, spent considerable time mapping the powerful existence of queer femininity. The fields of feminism and queer theory have also neglected her, the former dismissing her potential while the latter folds her signifiers into pure artifice. I hope to do something different in this chapter. "Strange Sisters" grows out of my reading of fem(me) performance cultures in Toronto by documenting and theorizing them as a new post-queer wave of representational practices and communities. These cultures, as traces of social movements, have not just surpassed queer and feminist representational practices and political ideas but also, as a 21st-century aesthetic avant-garde, thoroughly contests them at the same time.

These artists embody and depict what we might call the *queerest of the queer* in terms of social location; that is, through their performances they draw our attention to the simultaneity of queer femininity and racialized queer femininity as intersectional axes of power and resistance. In this chapter, I want to explore a few of these performances as what Hemmings, Duggan, and McHugh dub a new kind of "fem(me)inism," a set of post-queer, multicultural, third wave feminist texts emerging on the site of the community-based festival as a political site. These are post-queer, aesthetic, and representational ruptures made in one urban Canadian context (Toronto) in overlapping but different interdisciplinary and multimedia (literature, performance art, spoken-word, video, and visual performing arts) forms. Again, by using the term "post-queer," I argue that the available gender and sexual subjectivities within queer theory and within feminist, gay, lesbian, and bisexual paradigms are not extensive enough to account for these queerly feminine subjects who are sometimes trans-gendered, sometimes lesbian, sometimes queer, sometimes femmes of colour and, as a result, multimedia, post-colonial, and trans-genre in aesthetic methodologies. In other words, these are what José Esteban Muñoz's book, *Disidentifications: Queers of Colour and the Performance of Politics*, describes as queer feminist subjects who must dis-identify with the representations of multicultural heterosexual femininity but also dis-identify with White queer and lesbian representational practices (hence their simultaneous post-queer and post-colonial social positionings).

The work I can explore only briefly here spans approximately 10 years in the Toronto lesbian, feminist, trans-gender/trans-sexual, and queer artistic communities. Toronto is the context for aesthetic production, but more specifically, I want to pay homage to the performance/video/textual work of urban writers/poets, performance artists, festival curators, and video-makers who all converge on one primary festival site: a queer, post-colonial, performing arts cabaret known as "Strange Sisters," housed at Toronto's Buddies in Bad Times Theatre. The primary production work of curating the artists showcased in the "Strange Sisters" festival was completed by a high-profile individual in the Canadian cultural scene, Anna Camilleri (*Boys Like Her: Transfictions*; *Brazen Femme: Queering Femininity*, and the just-published, *I Am a Red Dress*), herself a performing artist and writer. An important group of artists performed in a cabaret called "Strange Sisters," which showcased artists thinking through feminist questions of queer and post-colonial femininity as lesbian subjectivity on that stage and sometimes in print. The performing, video, or arts festival (usually government funded) is itself an important cultural event that functions as a site for the construction and development of artistic, aesthetic, and community practices. Artists who have performed include Asian-Canadian Mariko Tamaki; queer working-class femme Zoe Whittall ("The Best 10 Minutes of Your Life" and "Geeks, Misfits and Outlaws"); northern B.C. short-story writer Ivan Coyote; spoken-word artists/poets Anurima Banerji, Dionne Brand, and Leah Lakshmi Piepzna-Samarasinha; Lebanese-Canadian poet Trish Salah ("Wanting in Arabic"); hip hop spoken-word poet/recording artist Motion (Wendy Brathwaite); Cuban-Canadian dub poet d'bi.young, and third wave feminist performance troupes like, for instance, "Pretty, Porky and Pissed Off." Many of these are third wave feminist, post-colonial, and queer performance artists and poets made their debut at "Strange Sisters," which became, in some cases, a community and communal writers' workshop. This work, as Peggy Phelan suggests, was also live performance and, as such, is sometimes non-recorded, contextual, and therefore extremely difficult to document and theorize as performance. The works showcased and the context of this festival are decidedly hybrid—feminist, queer, and post-colonial: the audience is equally hybrid with different ways of organizing sexual identities; the thematics of the performances and texts address complex questions of nationalisms (queer, lesbian, and racial) at the end of the 20th century; and the sexual politics address the specificities of being lesbian but feminine, racially marked but queer, and hybrid-Canadian and *Other* all at the same time.

Performances of queer femininity at the end of the twentieth century were not entirely uncommon in popular culture. One of my favourite television shows staged this precisely as a problematic albeit in less racially conscious ways. "I'm not a man," says Kristen Johnston, who plays Sally Solomon on the very popular NBC television show "3rd Rock from the Sun."[1] In the same interview, she elaborates: "People keep thinking a guy is playing Sally because she's so tough" (www.etonline.com). "3rd Rock from the Sun" is the successful sitcom that shows the acculturation processes of so-called aliens on a mission to earth. Sally Solomon, as the show's Web site tells us, "is second-in-command who is frustratingly reduced to what she considers to be an inferior role as a woman in today's society" (www.3rdrock.com/). The other aliens (Tommy, Dick, and Harry) also inhabit human bodies to materialize themselves without creating suspicion, bodies that are White, North American, able-bodied, thin, heterosexual, and seemingly appropriately gendered, although many of the sitcom's plot points spin around the less visible contradictions and paradoxes of these supposedly self-evident factualities. But with every character there emerges a state of virtual *hyper-trans-ness*: Tommy, the youngest member of the family, is actually, in alien terms, an old man crossing age difference to represent adolescence. Harry, marked as White, masculine, and kind of dumb, fails in his manliness yet still intelligently *out-mans* even the most hyper-masculine earth-male. Dick, like Tommy, crosses age difference and is easily both a five-year-old child and 17-year-old teenager trapped in the body—and, I suppose, mind—of a physics professor. Sally herself is, to turn an awkward phrase, *trans-genderedly hyper-feminine*, seemingly housed in a body from which she seems alienated and yet with which she is pleasurably surprised when "it" succeeds, as it often does, with heterosexual men in a "foreign" sexual economy. Misrecognitions of Johnston's performance as Sally seem to be accurately, if not unconsciously, discerning a contradiction at the heart of femininities at the end of the 20th century. That is, Sally is both femininity, overdetermined as body, supposedly ego- and agency-less, but also fem(me)ininity, with the enclosure of ego at the centre, a doubled enclosure, to quote Lisa Duggan and Kathleen McHugh, that recalls and ironically reiterates engendering truth regimes. Sally is, in other words, *trans-gendered* and ironic fem(me).[2]

Sally's *trans-gendered fem(me)ininity* raises compelling questions about femininity, questions that similarly overdetermine femininity on the site where it is thought to be the least self-evident and the most invisible; that is, on *queer* fem(me)ininity. In many ways, the relation between *trans-gender* and fem(me)ininity has been, to date, a *non-sequitur*. Trans-gender typically has marked a space of subjectivity that is in contradistinction from the body in which it finds itself. Historically derived from "transgenderist," the term has conventionally marked cross-gender living, which does not entail necessarily reconfiguring bodies with hormones and surgery (the space of trans-sexuality). In other words, the term now functions as what Jay Prosser (1997: 310) calls a container term, which includes a wide variety of gender outlaws: transvestites and cross-dressers, trans-sexuals, drag queens, butches, drag kings, bull dykes, androgynes, and intersexuals.

Interestingly, this somewhat telling list continues to foreground a wide variety of cross-gendered subjects, although persistently absented from the container is, of course, those who find themselves in the term "femme" as it emerges on what can be (mis-)read as a so-called successfully *naturalized* female body.[3] I belabour this question of definition for two reasons: first, because I want to reconceptualize femme subjectivity as *queerly trans-gendered*; and second, because I want to explore how the performance art of *queerly trans-gendered* femme artists reconfigure both fem(me)ininity and the processes by which fem(me) is desired, epistemologically *known* or (mis-)recognized, and, eventually, consumed through the gaze. As with Sally from "3rd Rock," a figure who does not appear to be queer but who is certainly high femme, the gaze is one of the primary producers of what is posited as the self-evident, but which remains, in practice at least, a conceptual overdetermination between what one thinks one is seeing and traces of essentialist and biologically determinist truth/knowledge regimes. In the case of fem(me)ininity, what one sees is not at all what one gets. The trick, for subjects of fem(me)ininity, is how to stage the gaze as a scene of that knowledge within an economy that simultaneously interpellates and discursively binds in the same looking relations. How, in other words, can fem(me)ininity resist precisely what femininity is articulated through and contained by?

What has conventionally been called "the gaze" has been extensively written about for almost 20 years in almost as many fields and disciplines. In her influential essay, "Visual Pleasure and Narrative Cinema," Laura Mulvey made one of the earliest interventions in theorizing the gaze when she argues that gendered power relations lie at the root of the gaze. Mulvey's (1989: 25) work theorizing narrative cinema suggests that the female image in film, woman's to-be-looked-at-ness, functions as the raw material for the active gaze of the man. "Going far beyond highlighting a woman's to-be-looked-at-ness," Mulvey (1989: 25) argues, "cinema builds the ways she is to be looked at into the spectacle itself." Men alone possess the gaze, women are to be looked at, and this active/passive heterosexual division of labour controls narrative structure (Mulvey 1989: 20). Conversely, as one of the active controllers of the gaze, the male spectator identifies with the main male protagonist while pleasure for female viewers is marked by visual transvestism (Mulvey 1981). That is, Mulvey resolves the "women in the audience issue" by suggesting that women actively identify across gender to enable a fantasy of masculinization in order to undo the masochism of her subject position (Mulvey 1989: 29).

> For women (from childhood onwards) transsex identification is a habit that very easily becomes second nature. However, this Nature does not sit easily and shifts restlessly in its borrowed transvestite clothes. (Mulvey 1989: 33)

For Mulvey, the gaze is always masculine and active; to-be-looked-at-ness always feminine and passive.

Many critics have deconstructed the essentialist and essentializing premises and implications of Mulvey's model of the gaze. But Evans and Gamman in particular take issue with the way in which Mulvey's argument both occludes ethnicity and a White gaze as well as the possibility of a female gaze in a historical moment different from her own. That is, it may well have been true in the 1970s that hyper-sexualized images of men were not available for consumption by both women and other men, but certainly no one could make that argument at the turn of the 20th century. Moreover, Mulvey's work renders invisible a White and colonial gaze almost innocuous, again a less than realistic implication. The focus on gender rather than ethnicity or race mirrors some early debates within feminist and queer theories that all but ignored the issue of race. So if Mulvey's work is so uncategorically limited, why reference her work at all?

As a structural model of the gaze, where both the spectator and text are decidedly fixed and foundational, Mulvey's scenario is uninteresting. However, when queered, destabilized from essentialist and biologically determinist arguments about gendered bodies and subjects, and unmoored from its structural foundations, Mulvey's model might allow us to theorize a productivity between the gaze and fem(me)ininities that allows for a rethinking of the work each accomplishes. That is, when combined with Berger's work on the gaze, these engendered dynamics of looking become quite interesting. At the very least, the gaze certainly implies far more than just looking at something; it signifies instead a complex relationship of power where, almost all critics agree, the gazer has a power over the object of the gaze. Berger's (1972: 45) *Ways of Seeing* codes this assumption directly into the work itself, observing that men act and women appear. Men look at women, he argues, while women watch themselves being watched (Berger 1972: 47). Women are, in other words, aware of being seen by a male spectator (Berger 1972: 49).

What's even more interesting about Berger's work is the dynamic he maps between a consciousness of visibility and resistance. Berger makes an important argument about the way the male gaze, especially in art, subjects women. Berger argues wonderfully in a complex treatise on looking in art and popular culture that there are socially manufactured differences in looking: first, masculinity watches, gazes, usually from a position of power and with a physical presence that almost always presumes power or the promise of power as almost three-dimensional: "A man presence suggests what he is capable of doing to you or for you …" (Berger 1972: 44–47). A woman, on the other hand, exists in a kind of fragmentation: to be a woman means to be born within the confines of an allotted and confined space. A woman, therefore, must continually watch herself. She is almost continually accompanied, as a result, Berger argues, by her own image of herself. She is both the surveyor and the surveyed. Berger (1972: 44–47) writes: "That part of a woman's self which is the surveyor treats the part which is the surveyed so as to demonstrate to others how her whole self would like to be treated … one might simplify this by saying: men act and women appear. Men look at women. Women watch themselves being looked at. This determines not only most relations between men and women but also the relation of women to themselves." The surveyor of women in herself is a male gaze internalized; the surveyed is female. Thus she turns herself into an object, particularly an object of vision.

So if, as both Berger and Mulvey and others suggest, looking is imbued with power, then in this formulation, women do the work of self-scrutinizing, policing, and regulating. This is clearly also what Mulvey is attempting to work through in a culture organized, at least in part, around these looking relations. Using psychoanalysis, Mulvey attempts to discover where and how the fascination of film is reinforced by pre-existing patterns of fascination and looking already at work in subjects, patterns produced by, in other words, cultural patterns or relations of looking in a social formation. In other words, film reflects, reveals, and plays on the socially manufactured relations of gender and desire. Mulvey wants to appropriate psychoanalysis as a political tool for theorizing these relations to suggest that there is a great deal more happening when we look as when we desire. To be put this into one sentence: she's arguing that structures of race and gender structure conventional Hollywood narrative fictional film.

But when reading the work of queer femmes, we cannot read the relationship between femme and femininity without also reading the work done between camp and irony. Irony has functioned in queer contexts as a form of camp, a critical reading and performance strategy. We associate the term "camp" with cross-dressing and other facets of queer culture. Yes, this is true but more accurately, camp describes a body of practices and strategies, including cross-dressing, drag, and ironic resignification, to resist biological and sexual essentialism about gender and sexuality as natural. These practices and strategies include filling the heteronormative gaze with spectacles that displace that gaze to challenge it. As a codification of those rejections, the processes of camp attempt to put the artifice of those systems on display through irony, masquerade, satire, parody, all of which share, of course, hyperbolization as a tactic. When camp works, it recodes and resignifies these ideologically inflected but also productive practices. So camp, in other words, offers transgressive strategies to invoke and parody the dominant ideological structures that render themselves invisible when they do their job properly.

Of course, camp has been a queer strategy, but with the performance texts under discussion here, we're starting to see a curious feminist appropriation of camp and parody as strategies of resistance to these very limited functions of the gaze. In her very interesting essay, "What Makes the Feminist Camp?" Pamela Robertson links feminist work on the gaze and looking relations with theories of camp to argue that if Mulvey's mapping of the male gaze is active, then strategic appropriations of camp, but especially this notion of masquerade through parody, can help alleviate this structural problem. What campish identifications enable, she argues, is that instead of a presumed overidentification with a passive image of self, camp entails assuming the mask of spectator to distance oneself from images to enable reading against the grain and to create an ironic distance between oneself and one's image. Camp offers, she suggests, a different model of negotiation for the "viewer," who now sees through simultaneous masks of seriousness and parodic femininity to open up new kinds of pleasure to a female spectator.

One of the very recent texts to camp queer femininity is, of course, Lisa Duggan and Kathleen McHugh's "The Fem(me)inist Manifesto" (1996). This manifesto is, like other manifestoes, an attempt to articulate, in the registers of hyperbole and with tremendous irony, a femme call to arms. The piece is written for femmes, directed as masculinity—in equal parts trans-, bio-, and female—with the goal of destabilizing and ironizing exactly what we mean by the term "femme." Their choice of spelling—fem(me)—is deliberate and works against the self-effacing imperatives of femininity; that is, the spelling, like the spelling of "boi," works as a performative to signal distance and rupture from the referent each modifies. This manifesto maps economies of resistance, rendering femininity hyper-performative and strangely defamiliarized. In fact, each of these performance texts that I will consider here signifies or performs some kind of violence: the Duggan and McHugh feminist camp manifesto, like any manifesto, shatters the reader's habituated thought patterns and overfamiliarity by jarring us into an entirely different stylization of the word. Manifestoes, as a public declarative form, make manifest or visible that which habituated thought puts under erasure and, by necessity, are characterized by elevated diction and tone. Curiously, the term comes from the Latin *manu festus* or "struck by hand," implying the shock of that strike as one way to get attention.

Reading the "Fem(me)inist Manifesto" (FM) as camp manifesto allows us to read its violence as less literal and, I would argue, more formal. That is, beyond the sexual ambiguities implied by "struck by hand," the subject of FM deliberately plays on the spaces between categories: she is both and fully neither lesbian nor heterosexual; she becomes the source of power in the scene by inhabiting normal abnormally; she establishes the narrative frame in the opening, reminding us that this is a fantasy, but is also the subject of the now hyper-real scene of fantasy. "She" cannot be known and hence contained in categories; her articulations exist in both narrative levels and in both sexual subjectivities (that is, both lesbian femme and heterosexual femme fatale all at the same time). It is precisely her control of what's intelligible or knowable situated as it is within what she knows is unintelligible for masculinity, which allows the narrative to unfold the way it does.

These two authors do precisely what I suggest FtM subjects do; they take a fairly specific subject position—that is, in this case, lesbian femme, and universalize the qualities of that subject; signifiers (femininity as clothing, as performance, as stylization of the body, as attitude, as sexual power, as desiring of masculinity) in that universalization become radically disconnected from the female and, by implication, heteronormative female body. This, they argue, is mixed up with the best of girl power, camp, the best of postmodern irony and performativity, and consequently our former subject has become transformed into a queer feminine superhero that anyone of any gender or sexuality can inhabit. They put it so much better than I: "Within postmodernism, the fem(me) reappears, signifier of another kind of gender trouble. Not a performer of legible gender transgression, like the butch or his sister the drag queen, but a betrayer of legibility itself. Seemingly 'normal,' she responds to 'normal' expectations with a sucker punch—she occupies normality abnormally" (Duggan and McHugh 1996: 108). Occupying normality abnormally is a prescription for resistance. These are women who are not shamed by the performative terms "slut," "bitch," "ball buster," and so on, but by transforming the context of their use, transform how and what they signify, inhabiting them to turn them against the way that these words are used to contain. Duggan and McHugh call this a fem(me) science in order to suggest that when one can answer the question of what something is, one then has the power to define categories, essences, and knowledge systems. Part of what is at stake here is the political use of irony as strategy of resistance in which femininity works against the systems that give it meaning. They write: "Fem(me)inity steals the show (she is the show) of difference, but she cannot be fixed as a certain effect in itself [...] Mirrors are not the pool in which she drowns; they are the instrument of her essential irony" (Duggan and McHugh 1996: 107).

In her article, "Out of Sight, Out of Mind? Theorizing Femme Narrative," Clare Hemmings (1999) also explores irony as a productive disruptor of the gaze. Hemmings revisits late 19th-century sexology to argue that, from its inception, the logic of sexology has failed to fully articulate the feminine invert. Either the feminine invert, who has failed in her femininity by passively receiving the attentions of the wrong object (that is, the masculine woman), will "cure" or redeem the blight on her femininity by returning to the "real" heterosexual male or she has always already failed in her femininity because she is in the category that Havelock Ellis describes as "women whom the average man would pass by" (quoted in Hemmings 1999: 452). In either scenario, she remains bound by suspicions; either her heterosexuality is compromised or her supposedly natural femininity is compromised. The only other option that sexology provides, Hemmings argues, is curious: "Ellis's construction [of the feminine invert] raises the possibility that, given their status as objects of masculine attention, all heterosexuality-bound women have the capacity to commit the same 'error' of mistaking the masculine invert's attention for 'the real thing'" (Hemmings 1999: 452). Thus, argues Hemming, rather than resolving the problem of the feminine invert, Ellis universalizes the problem as constitutive of *all* femininities.

> While the femme may continue to be haunted by her "inevitable return to heterosexuality," heterosexual femininity itself is scarcely free of perversion, but remains haunted in turn by the possibility of seduction by the masculine woman. (Hemmings 1999: 453)

Hemmings's argument puts flesh on Butler's rethinking of the relations between sexuality and gender in the sex/gender system. That is, Hemmings's reading of femininity posits that sexuality works against gender to let that which cannot fully appear in any performance of fem(me)ininity persist in its dis-ruptural promise (Butler 1991: 29).

These femme interruptions leave the house of femininity in a state of disarray. Such a position, as Hemmings (1999: 453) herself notes, leaves the feminine woman structurally positioned as subject to both a heterosexual and queer "male" gaze, and while femininity is conferred and consumed in those sexualizing gazes, it is also true that one cannot tell, just by looking, which, if either, gaze she might return. Femininity and, by implication, her *queer-ing* cousin fem(me)ininity, is thus a perception of a successful naturalization of discourses of femininity, especially when those discourses are naturalized on what is also conventionally presumed to be a female body and especially when the effect is to receive and similarly naturalize a heterosexualizing male gaze.

Hemmings makes some important theoretical observations about femininity as well as the one suggested in the quote above. She suggests, for example, that "femininity is conferred upon [a woman] though the masculine gaze" (Hemmings 1999: 453). Hemmings is responding to the way a crisis of visuality around fem(me)ininity has been named in queer theory and performed in queer fiction and performance art. Given that many of the visual signifiers of femininity are the same for both heterosexual and queer feminine subjects, in representational contexts queer fem(me)ininity can often pass as heterosexual femininity. In narrative terms, as Hemmings (1999: 455) argues, this means that the femme is invisible as a queer sexual subject once she is out of the sight of, or does not return, masculinity's gaze. Or, to phrase this the way Teresa de Lauretis did in 1993 when she responded to the concerns that Esther Newton raised in 1989 about *the feminine invert*, "in most representational contexts, [femme is] either passing lesbian or passing straight, her (homo)sexuality being in the last instance what cannot be seen. Unless […] she enter the frame of vision *as* or *with* a lesbian in male body drag" (de Lauretis 1993: 155; emphasis in original). The notion that femme represents an occlusion, an articulate silence hailed by a masculine gaze, suggests that fem(me)ininity can also refuse or repudiate that same gaze. Such refutations and refusals are the very *stuff* of the performance art by Anna Camilleri and Machiko Saito, who, in performative reiterations of *trans-gendered* femininity and fem(me)ininity, stage the scene of the gaze only to render it and its conditions of possibility impotent.[4]

But we also need to tweak our notions of the gaze. If we have been arguing that engendering processes occur through looking relations, then it might be equally possible to suggest that racialization—that is, the placement of subjects into supposedly self-evident categories of race—also occurs when we look. If the subject of femininity is subjected by, but is also attempting to be outside of the ideology of gender, if this subject is split and contradictory as de Lauretis (1987: 10) suggests, and if feminism needs to organize through what I described earlier as de Lauretis's space-off or blind spot of discourse, then what might that space-off look like within or inside racialized genders? We can no longer speak, as we've been doing, in absolutes about this fictional creature "woman" or "femme" without precision in location. That is, as many queer women of colour have suggested, feminism needs to create new spaces of discourse, to rewrite cultural narratives, and to define the terms of another perspective. De Lauretis (1987: 25) calls this the view from elsewhere, or the view from the margins of hegemonic discourse, its space-offs and blind spots: "the spaces in the margins of hegemonic discourses, social spaces carved in the interstices of institutions and in the chinks and cracks of the power-knowledge machine." All of the texts in this book share at least one assumption: that it's time, long overdue, in fact, to shift the terms of our debates. That shift is not to anti-feminist positions. Instead, the focus shifts from theorizing *differences from* approaches—that is, women's differences *from* men or queers *from* heterosexuals—toward a deconstruction of each category itself. So instead of a *differences from* strategy, we need to see from a perspective that looks for *differences within.*

To put this differently, if Berger argued that femininity is defined and constituted by that gaze from men (defined in terms of her visibility, she carries her own Panopticon[5] with her wherever she goes, her self-image a function of her being for another) then it certainly might also be true that being a woman (and likely a man too but for now, woman) of colour, marked by race, might mean to similarly be split between the image and the self, the watcher and the watched. That is, if women need a gendered oppositional gaze, then women of colour also need still another oppositional reading practice within these categories themselves (hooks 1992: 130). Part of the crisis mapped for us then is one of categories and the overdetermined but unmarked White complexion of our universal categories. So, femmes of colour are doubled in categories and in the impossible space-off of each world: the categories of gender and sexuality but also the categories of race, if not, at times, also the categories of class. The result, as Muñoz indicates (1999), is a dis-identifying subject position, an in-between, liminal identity seemingly contradictory but bound within ideologies of race, sexuality, class, and gender as they overlap, and in the space-off of each other. This seems to bear out Berger's assertion even though we've modified it; women of colour watch themselves be watched and carry around with them that idea of who they should be and then become, as Berger suggested, both the surveyor (the watcher) and the surveyed (the watched), only this is layered with both race and gender simultaneously.

We also see this play out in the work of Machiko Saito, an Asian-American, San Francisco-based, experimental video artist. She has worked as an actor in theatre, film, and television, and has directed a number of her own solo performances in San Francisco and New York. Machiko is also creator, director, producer, editor, and host of the San Francisco late-night variety show "Femme TV." She is also the director, editor, and producer of three short films: the award-winning *Premenstrual Spotting* (1997, 12 mins.); *15 Minutes of Femme* (1998, 15 mins.), and her latest, *Pink Eye* (2000, 7 mins.). A testament to the dialogism of the signifiers of femininity and fem(me)ininity, her work has been programmed at a very diverse and wide variety of independent film festivals such as Tranny Fest 1997 and again in 1998; The Tampa International Gay and Lesbian Film Festival 2000; San Francisco International Film Festival; Prostitution and Sex Work: Sex Worker Film and Video Festival 1999; Inside/Out: The Toronto International Lesbian and Gay Film and Video Festival 2000[6]; and 2000 Black Maria Film Festival, produced by the Media Arts Department of New Jersey City University.

Saito's style is formally experimental and visually vertiginous, with image after image sutured together to produce a collage/montage of compelling images that are also profoundly troubling. In the two videos included as part of the *Inside/Out* Femme Frenzy program—*Premenstrual Spotting* (*PMS*) and *15 Minutes of Femme* (*15 MF*)—both of which are about 15 minutes in length, the content and rapidity of images work against that "short" time frame to shake the viewer out of narrative time and space. Saito herself works behind the camera as producer, writer, and editor and in front of the camera as performer, the effect of which is to blur distinctions between autobiography or memoir and fiction, a technique very common in much contemporary butch-femme and gender "outlaw" writing. However, where much identity-based narrative prose and film/video produces, however contingently, stable subjects with at least the appearance of core subjectivity, Saito's work marks a radical point of departure from a positive images school of representation and moves rapidly toward destabilizing the representational and erotic gazes through which fem(me)ininities are often articulated.

Such destabilizations are not easily accomplished. *15 MF* is a complex short video that initially seems as if it is "merely" a representational montage of the diverse San Francisco queer and trans-gender community. Leading with clips from the San Francisco gay pride march, *15 MF* skips through opening studio shots of Saito, then bars, bar bathrooms, and change rooms/closets, and finally more studios shots of Saito performing before the video lands on what are more identifiably quasi-narrative clips from the San Francisco television show, "Femme TV." The clips suture together a collage of queer gender performances across race, genders, body types, and some discernibly *trans-gendered* bodies. Saito appears in the opening prefatory studio shots as "Miss LaMay," host of "Femme TV" and high femme dominatrix, dressed in high-heeled boots, long black dress, and corset worn outside the dress. All of the images of Saito/Miss LaMay are dialogic in the sense that they evoke multiple signifiers of both gender and race simultaneously. Saito's identity as an Asian woman becomes performative when she wears, as she often does, either chopsticks or plastic knives and forks in her hair. Chopsticks are overdetermined signifiers in North America, and the signifiers of race invite and similarly destabilize a White orientalist gaze as often as a male gaze.

In case there is any question of who controls these dialogic and simultaneous images of Asian and queer fem(me)ininities, Miss LaMay wields a television remote control in each hand and after introducing the protocols ("Basically, here's how it works at 'Femme TV.' I follow an idea or see something that catches my attention, and I put it on the air."), she clicks one and activates the images that the viewer sees. At this point, she then permits the viewer to look at the by now meta-textual images of fem(me)ininity, which include Saito herself emerging from behind the camera to ask questions of her subjects. We do not actually hear the dialogue but only see its formal properties: smiles upon recognitions, mouths moving, hands gesturing greetings and obscenities at the camera as it consumes the signifiers of femininity (hair, bodies, faces wearing makeup, fetish-wear and high femme clothing and highly stylized footwear). Instead, a sound track of electronic music provides accompaniment until the final quasi-narrative segment in which the song "All That Jazz" accompanies the images to articulate the genders through a vertiginous and (gender) troubling irony.

But Saito also appears in an embedded performance right before the Miss LaMay segment. This performance is very short, lasting about 10 seconds, and is another series of studio shots that sets up the work that the final narrative segment accomplishes. In these studio shots, Saito is performing naked, wearing only high-heeled shoes. But again, the camera fetishes the fragments of the feminine body, which are anything but self-evident or natural as signifiers: breasts, feet in shoes, heavily made-up face, and highly stylized hair held off the body with either chopsticks or plastic knives and forks, red lips smoking a cigarette. However, in the same instant that these signifiers articulate femininity, Saito *de-articulates* the Asian female body by covering it with black duct tape: the camera slows down as she tears each piece of tape off the roll and covers her vulva lips, breasts, mouth, and, finally, eyes. All that remains unbound are her hands, which continue to hold a lit cigarette. The effect of the performance is stunning: where the female body was overdetermined, signifying prolifically, now its self-imposed binding refuses signification and truncates the camera's consumption of those signifiers. As if to enact Butler's (1993: 5) delimitation of "sex" in the rhetoric of the sex/gender system, Saito frustrates femininity's identifications with *to-be-looked-at-ness* by de-articulating a corporeality overburdened by signification. That is, the body that matters here is one that refuses coherence through the engendering terms of the gaze. This is a body that overloads a representational specular economy, one that binds fem(me)ininities to, by, and with the female body although it refuses simultaneously to put that body on display for the gaze. If, as Martin (1996: 73) has suggested, within a queer aesthetic practice "the feminine, played straight, cannot appear unless it is camped up or disavowed, constituting a capitulation, a swamp, something maternal, ensnared and ensnaring," then Saito's work in this brief performance begins to articulate a fem(me)ininity grounded in a performative muting of that previously determinist corporeality. This is not a queerly gendered body conceptualized in negative terms—that is, as an escape from gender or dis- and re-embodiment of itself. Rather, what becomes visible is a body refusing the terms of conceptualization by productively de-articulating itself from a gaze that fixes the female body as a coherent body. This is fem(me)ininity playing (straight), but also as incoherence, as femininity unmarking itself in economies of *différence* as not reducible to its supposed biological destiny: this is fem(me)ininity as anti-foundationalist, *trans*-gendered refusal of engendering and corporealizing technologies like the gaze.

The final minutes of *15 MF* accomplish the work of performatively refusing and eventually assassinating that by now frustrated and destabilized masculine gaze that wants to look away but cannot. The stakes of looking now become those of life and death. The final scenes of *15 MF* murderously enact that refusal by staging a scene between two lovers, a butch and a femme, that becomes deadly. As if to create two parallel worlds, this scene is foiled with another that shows two trans-gendered femmes frolicking in front of the camera. These particular femmes are marked with dialogic signifiers of hyper-, and at times, unreal, fem(me)ininity: highly stylized wigs and clothing, fetish-thigh-high boots, heavy makeup, and, for one femme, doll-eyes contact lenses. Where one would expect the camp of the soundtrack's "All That Jazz" to inform this site of femininity, one finds instead virtual silence. "All That Jazz" menaces and eventually ironizes the butch-femme lovers instead. Its lyrics suggest that the imagined audience for this video is feminine as does the division of power (and labour) in the butch-femme sex scene. We first see the butch character staring off into space, seemingly waiting for the femme to come home. The femme finally appears through the door and the butch ingratiates himself to please her. They take to a bed, and kiss quite passionately. At this point, presumably after realizing that he is inadvertently wearing lipstick transferred in the kiss, the butch goes to the closet, pulls out feminine clothing, and begins to transform himself into a very campy-looking femme. Seemingly put off by this transformation, the femme goes to her closet and similarly transforms herself into a boy. In the midst of the gender-fuck clothing exchange, the camera jump-cuts to a poster on the wall that says, "Fuck Your Gender Happiness." For all intents and purposes, *she* is now butch to *his* femme.

Strangely, this reversal does not dramatically change the power relations between them. The new fem(me) retains the power to choreograph the sexual play, even though the butch is much more demonstrative in his actions. After some rough play, the fem(me) begins to top the butch with intense aggression and after they both take off their clothing, the femme begins to fuck the butch's mouth with the dildo. "She" continues fucking "him" quite violently until blood spills from his mouth and he appears lifeless. All action stops, the camera closes in on the femme's face as "she" stares incredulously at the lifeless body of masculinity. The music has stopped and after a few moments, the femme gets up, dresses, and leaves the apartment. Credits roll on a black screen until we have one final look at the lifeless shell of masculinity. There can be no doubt that this is a particularly devastating scene to watch. The reversal of gender leaves more questions asked than answered: If the previous scene, as I argued above, separates fem(me)ininity from the supposedly naturalized female body, then how do we read the genders performed in the butch-femme scene? Are we to understand that the femme does indeed represent fem(me)ininity and the butch masculinity? If yes, then does fem(me)ininity then possess the gaze in the end after masculinity is symbolically killed? If indeed the body is no longer the guarantee of gender, then why have these two gendered subjects exaggerate their gender performances? Why, in other words, camp or king up the gender performances in order to reverse the gaze? Do these exaggerations foreground, as Butler might suggest, the discursive idealizations of gender to again emphasize that argument that every embodied imitation is a failure in one way or another? If this is true, as I suggest with Butler that it is, then what is it about our epistemological constructions of gender and sexuality that continue to invest in fem(me)ininity as a successful naturalization (read: normalization) of those ideals? Could that assumption/ accusation of naturalization be the site of the queer *femme* rage performed here? Given the audience for Saito's work in the film festivals I referenced earlier, to whom is the message "Fuck your gender happiness" addressed: To so-called naturalized heterosexual men and women? Conventional (non-trans-gendered or trans-sexual) gay men and lesbians? To butches? To femmes? To trans-sexual men? Whose gender happiness is being quite literally fucked? With irony, to the essentialist presumption that *femme* equals *gender happiness*? Or, is it, as Duggan and McHugh (1996: 157) suggest, a staged scene where fem(me)ininity defeats and finally transcends the burden of the "natural," the "normal," and the feminine ("… ego-less, tolerant of, and therefore complicit with deception") of sexual difference as the masculine gaze has articulated it? This is the work of the gaze failing to cohere, masculinity ruptured again.

Saito is not from Toronto, but her work was screened by Camilleri and Brushwood Rose in the "Femme Frenzy" program of the Inside/Out Gay and Lesbian Film and Video Festival to some controversy. The entire program was a brave exploration of femme where she appears, as Duggan and McHugh put it, across genders. That is, videos in the program looked at femme in lesbian contexts, but also across different kinds of bodies, including self-identified male bodies. A number of these pieces, in different forms, appeared in the work *Brazen Femme: Queering Femininity* (Camilleri and Brushwood Rose 2002). Alongside Lesléa Newman's *The Femme Mystique* (1995), some of the pieces share commonalities with other anthologies, like, for instance, *The Persistent Desire: A Femme-Butch Reader* (1992), edited by Joan Nestle, and *Butch/Femme: Inside Lesbian Gender* (1998), edited by Sally Munt. But *Brazen Femme (BF)* ups the ante on these earlier works in a couple of significant ways. First, these earlier works, along with *A Restricted Country* by Joan Nestle, break ground by drawing our attention not only to butch-femme but also by challenging the often misogynistic readings of femme as a sidekick, a "helpmate," an appendage to masculinity. Second, though, *BF* links femme to femininity in one of the interesting shifts of allegiance and alliance that Sedgwick maps. In fact, *BF* posits the argument that even while femme rearticulates femininity, there is a line of continuity between femme and femininity that is full of interruptions. Still, femme is, as Camilleri and Brushwood Rose (2002: 13) write in the introduction, femininity gone wrong, the trappings of femininity gone awry. The terms, then, of femme, are both redress and pleasure (Camilleri and Brushwood Rose 2002: 13), but the stakes of pleasure here are, as we have already seen, fatal. Finally, then, this queer and queering rage marks *BF* as quite different from its predecessors. While being subjected by the gaze is a consistent part of femme experience (signalled on the cover of *Femme Mystique* as a femme attempting to return the gaze through a compact mirror), here seeing is the tithe, the price paid for an audacious gaze. *BF*'s cover image and its return to an earlier photograph from Camilleri's prior work, *Boys Like Her*, challenge the gaze with a knife: "I dared the viewer, the imagined viewer, to look. My legs spread apart, knife gripped tightly, mediating access. Seeing is the tithe, not the prize. A brazen posture? Yes" (Camilleri 2002: 11). This reading of the cover image mediates the introduction itself, gesturing like Berger's fragmented "woman" doubly, both to a femme look, already doubled relative to femininity, but also to what's about to unfold in the book itself: these moments of fragmentation gesture to a productive categorical im/possibility—incoherence—that refuses closure: "What cannot be seen, what cannot be held or pinned down, is where femme is" (Camilleri 2002: 12). She is not either side of the knife blade; she is its edge: "Femme is the blade—fatally sharp; a mirror reflecting back fatal illusions" (Camilleri 2002: 12). The violence of that edge is the redress and the pleasure.

It is no accident at all that Saito's work was curated by Camilleri. Each shares a relationship to this edge as it meets and slices through the gaze. Formerly a member of the performance troupe Taste This (Anna Camilleri, Ivan E. Coyote, Zoë Eakle, and Lyndell Montgomery) Camilleri's work was collected and published as *Boys Like Her: Transfictions (BLH)*. She is now based in Toronto and continues to write and present spoken-word performances. *Boys Like Her* (1998) is a collection of writings from tours and performances from Taste This, who identify across the spectrum of gender identities. One of the central tensions of Camilleri's work, both in *BLH* and since, is the representational imperatives and yet impossibilities of fem(me)ininities in both queer and trans contexts. That is, the subtitle of the collection—*Transfictions*—foregrounds the form of the work (fictions) and the location of the performers (trans), including Camilleri. The boys of the troupe (Ivan and Lyndell) are marked as trans by virtue of their cross-gendering; Zoë messes up all of the categories, but Anna's work is all too easily misread as the foundation, the ground, the fixity around which the other categories intersect, cross-sect, and dissect. Indeed, what productive gender trouble ensues when we ask: Is fem(me)ininity a necessary *Other* to the epistemologies of trans subjectivities? Is there an alternative re-(de)construction of *trans* that might allow what has been previously occluded to function as the categorical mark?

Consistent with the fem(me) dialogism in Saito's work, there are also multiple "Annas" in *BLH*. From the pun in the title (boys like or desire her), which is printed over a group photograph in which Camilleri's face is most prominent, through the sexual geometrics and triangles mapped in pieces like "Sweet Boy" (this story was penned by Anna, Ivan, and Lyndell and maps the gendered sexual dynamics of the affair between Anna and Ivan and the relationship between Lyndell and Anna), fem(me)ininity is centralized in this performance setting grounded in the ironies of many different gazes. "Mirrors are not the pool in which she drowns; they are the instrument or metaphor of her essential irony," write Duggan and McHugh (1996: 154). In *BLH*, subjectivities and gendered desire function as mirrors, especially for fem(me)ininities whose gaze itself is already doubled and who, as Berger (1972: 47) suggests, "watch themselves being looked at."

What those mirrored reflections, deflections, and refractions reveal is, of course, the ironies of the socially constructed face of femininity, from which fem(me)ininities are redoubled. One of Camilleri's pieces, "Skin to Scar," commands that gaze to attend to the processes by which her face was rebuilt when medically necessary and non-cosmetic surgeries became cosmetic. "Look at me," the voice insists:

Look carefully. Do you see my face? My totally asymmetrical face? My nose is clinically described as a deviated septum. My mandible and maxilla aren't perfectly lined up, and X-rays show that my chin is connected to my jaw with wire. Yes, I'm a head injury patient and a beautiful one at that. A beautifully built woman—I have the doctors to thank for that. [...] They did a wonderful job, don't you think? [...] Look at me [...] This face was rebuilt. (Camilleri et al. 1998: 88–89)

The gaze is welcomed through the first "Look at me." That invitation becomes a reiterative imperative by the time the second "Look at me" repeats. The double-sightedness that watches from two places at once—from within and from without—watches the watchers to display essentializing and naturalizing Girl-by-Nature machineries (Duggan and McHugh 1996: 154). Camilla Griggers calls these technologies the abstract-machine of faciality, a process in which the face represents an apparatus that, like a machine, constantly produces and reproduces the subject through the signifiers the apparatus requires. The face, in other words, is not a natural extension of the flesh, nor is it a signifier of an individuated consciousness. Rather, it is a signifying mechanism, a network of interpretations organizing a zone of acceptable expressions of the signifier and acceptable conductions of meanings to signs and of signs to social subjects (Griggers 1997: 3). Subjectivization is facialization. Femininity is then overcoded, abstract faciality where the face is a textual space in which meanings can be allowed to proliferate and resonate. The primary means through which this visual regime of signs is produced and consumed is, of course, through the gaze. Camilleri documents this facializing machine in action:

Beautiful. Yes beautiful. [...] These words repeat. [...]The surgeries were needed for medical reasons—and there were "cosmetic benefits." And this, the cosmetic benefits, is what seemed to excite and intoxicate the doctors more than anything else. I remember the calculated, hungry look in the eyes of surgeons who saw me the way an architect might view a partially constructed building. "Lovely foundation, it's a shame that it's not finished." They saw me as incomplete, unfinished and potentially beautiful. And what greater gift could a doctor give to this world than one more beautiful woman? (Camilleri et al. 1998: 91)

But, as Griggers also suggests, there is a way in which faciality can become *de-faced*. Becoming de-faced is to come into the transformational potential of the legacies constituting contemporary feminine social experiences without nostalgia for lost identities of the past and without illusions about the future. Griggers (1997: x) suggests that *becoming-woman* means to "enter the flows of matter and signs that have made up the turbulent and proliferating histories of the feminine [...] and to understand the delimited yet real possibilities for transformation that those histories afford." Becoming-woman, as Camilleri echoing Duggan and McHugh suggests, means to allow the doubled gaze of fem(me)ininity to sound the death knell or to de-face femininity (Duggan and McHugh 1996: 154). "Seemingly normal," Duggan and McHugh (1996: 155) argue, "she is a betrayer of legibility itself [...] she responds to 'normal' expectations with a sucker punch—she occupies normality abnormally." Camilleri deploys a similar rhetoric of strategic essentialism to show how fem(me)ininities are grafted from femininity, a so-called source that imagines itself as the original:

> None of the doctors ever asked me how I felt about my face. Go ahead, ask me now .... How do I feel? I can say this: I grew these bones myself, muscle to tendon, skin to cheek. I pushed myself into this world. (Camilleri et al. 1998: 92)

That so-called original (yet another assemblage) *loses face* and is even *effaced* in a politic that is ironically played out in the *trans-gendered* threshold between the perceptible and the imperceptible, and between the imaginary body and the flesh (Hart 1998: 10).

However, in the process of becoming-fem(me)ininity, Camilleri, like Saito, refuses to let that gaze remain unscathed and coherent, especially when that gaze imagines itself to be outside the field of vision in the so-called Real. That is if, as Mulvey (1989) suggests, gazing foregrounds a reading practice where masculinity identifies and femininity both identifies and dis-identifies, then Camilleri's story "Super Hero" stages a violent reversal of those subject-forming identificatory practices. "Super Hero" is a fantasy story that the nameless narrator gives herself very late one night when she is unable to sleep. "Furious, pounding, screaming inside," writes the narrator, "I know, mean and nasty thoughts aren't going to get me to sleep, but tonight I can't just do some deep breathing [....] No, tonight is different" (Camilleri 1998: 131). That difference is one in which the speaker recreates a common experience for women. The mise-en-abyme, already now twice removed from the real, puts a woman, late at night at the end of her shift, at a bus stop waiting for public transit, harassed by man after man (the "drive-bys") in cars, feeling, as the story suggests, like a sitting duck.

Those "mean and nasty thoughts," we soon discover, necessitate meeting and returning the gaze of one of the drive-bys as he follows the woman down the street, yelling obscenities out his van window. But unlike Mulvey's passive "to-be-looked-at-ness," the woman in this story allows the gaze to imagine it has accomplished its work of consuming femininity. Manipulating the desire of "Dick," the drive-by in the van, the woman climbs into his van, plays seductive and coy, and convinces him to return to her place. Once inside, the woman makes Dick comfortable and retreats to the bathroom to prepare. After she returns from the bathroom and pours a drink, the reader understands exactly what is occurring:

> I pour one shot of Scotch, quietly sort through my cabinet and gather my props. Dick is looking out the window. I hand him the drink and run my index finger down his chest. He smirks and takes a swig. I smile back broadly and bring my right kneecap sharply into his groin. Dick grabs his cock and crashes to his knees [....] While he's still down, I cuff him, kick him onto his belly and hogtie him [....] A beautiful sight. (Camilleri et al. 1998: 133)

Like Saito's visual and formal assault on the gaze, Camilleri's "Super Hero" watches the watcher watching and then makes the scene so unbearable that the watcher stops watching and looks elsewhere, all of which is witnessed (by the watched) from two places (both within and without) simultaneously. After tormenting Dick, reminding him that he has only himself to thank for the position he is in, and after reiterating his powerlessness, the woman, who introduces herself as Anna, duct tapes his keys between his shoulder blades and throws him out of her apartment and watches him stumble down the street naked.

> I walk over to my window, light a cigarette and watch the smoke scatter as it hits the pane. The streetlight is buzzing more loudly than usual. Halfway through my cigarette, Dick stumbles out of my building. He's buck-naked, hunching over, trying to cover his cock. (Camilleri et al. 1998: 135)

The text is accompanied by a photograph of a woman sitting, photographed from the neck down. The woman is seated with her legs pulled up to reveal black leather boots with a very thick high heel, legs clad in stockings held up by a garter belt, arms clasping her knees to her chest, with her only visible hand clutching a knife blade. This image of her body as signifier now draws attention to itself as that which remains, like the image of the knife, in excess of the male gaze. That is, the appearance of the female body is that object that was produced by the gaze and that is now the same subject functioning in excess of that same gaze. The gaze that once functioned to secure meaning has simultaneously displaced/deferred the fixed meaning of that signifier and fails to reproduce the corporeal referent. The gaze, in other words, is mirrored back onto itself.

The fem(me)ininity in performance, both textually and when Camilleri performs "Super Hero," stages the failure of the signifiers of femininity to secure a relation between subjectivity and the so-called female body *qua* body. In the earlier bathroom mirror scene, Camilleri stages the female gaze as performative and productively self-naming through ritualized speech-acts.

> I lock the bathroom door behind me. I look in the mirror and see myself:
> a bitch-femme. My eyes are hard and dilated. [...] I run my tongue slowly
> along sharp teeth. I silently call on all of the bold bitch-femmes who have
> come before me, to be here, now. (Camilleri et al. 1998: 132–133)

The double-sightedness of fem(me)ininity, which stages a violent assault on both the gaze and the signifiers it productively consumes, does so for both Camilleri and Saito from within a number of places at once: "woman," "bitch," "whore/dominatrix," and "queer." The male gaze is dependent upon both visibility but also a coherent point of view that provides it with the cloaked machineries of objectification. In the ironically titled "Super Hero," in "Skin to Scar," but also in *15 Minutes of Femme*, that point of view is radically destabilized and shattered, as are the machineries upon which it depends. If Foucault (1982: 64) is correct when he argues that "the agency of domination does not reside in the one who speaks (for it is he who is constrained), but in the one who listens [or watches] and says nothing," then for Camilleri and Saito, those relations of power operative in the gaze are inverted when it is the silent and split spectator of fem(me)ininity who watches a performance of femininity dominate and control the visual exchanges.

These tensions are raised by *BLH*, but it isn't until we get to *I Am a Red Dress: Incantations on a Grandmother, a Mother, and a Daughter*, that the dis-ruptural potential of Camilleri's project is fully actualized. *Red Dress* is, as the subtitle suggests, a series of incantations on femininity as it triangulates through three generations of women, where femininity is continuously interrupted by femme, which does not take shape until the final generation. Lyrical, poetic, and elegiac in places, *Red Dress* maps that trajectory beautifully. The grammar or lexicon of *Red Dress* are the realities of women's lives, the most potent of which is the consistent sexual abuse of girl children by a maternal grandfather. Structured by what each generation cannot know about itself—grandmother, mother, daughter—*Red Dress* introduces us to the daughter, "Annina," violently raped by the grandfather for years, as she comes to embody, as femme, the unthinkable rage of each generation of women before her. While Annina's experiences are the same, her choices are not. As a femme who comes of age, she files charges against her grandfather, who is imprisoned for his violence.

The book's red cover design signals that incantation. Annina's mother repeats an imperative that she herself is unable to actualize: "When your grandfather dies I'm going to the funeral in a red dress" (Camilleri 2004: 115). This as possibility repeats endlessly throughout the text like a frustrated desire. "Wearing anything but black to a funeral, to my father's funeral—now that would be a disgrace," her mother confesses. "A red dress is for parties, for celebration" (Camilleri 2004: 96). But for the young Annina, that desire and its tenacity mark the space between femininity and femme. That is, coded into what each generation cannot know—where each is cut from the same hard stone—are the templates for the next generation's work and, in this case, a post-queer third wave fem(me)inist imperative:

> This story is a lexicon between my grandmother, my mother, and I—the stuff that mythology is made of—mother, maiden, and crone. Grandmother notices a red dress. Mother imagines wearing a red dress. Daughter becomes the red dress. The redress. (Camilleri 2004: 12).

NOTES

1. A Carsey-Werner production.

2. This particular formation, which combines femme and femininity to manifest the relation and yet the *différence* of these two subjects, comes from Lisa Duggan and Kathleen McHugh's "A Fem(me)inist Manifesto," *Women & Performance: A Journal of Feminist Theory* 8:2 (1996): 107-110.

3. The term "naturalized" describes an effect of engendering. While usually referring to a performative moment where an immigrant is conferred Canadian or indeed any national citizenship, I use it here to reference a similar performative reading practice that infers a body type based on a (mis-)reading of a gender performance, one that is assumed to have emerged naturally out of that body.

4. Ultimately, this chapter challenges the assumptions behind the descriptor "trans-gendered," which might argue that to be trans-gendered, one's subjectivity must be the opposite gender of one's body. I am certainly not suggesting that either of these two *individuals* are necessarily personally trans-gendered; rather I am attempting to expand the conceptualization of the term "trans-gendered" to mark subjectivities that are differently dis-embodied and to trouble the way the concept privileges hyper-visibility for some of its subjects (MtF and FtM trans-sexuals; butch-boys; trans-gendered boys and girls, etc.) and invisibility for others (for instance, lesbian-femmes).

5. This, of course, is not Berger's concept. I borrow the term "panopticon" from Foucault's *Discipline and Punish: The Birth of the Prison* (1977).

6. Saito's works were screened as part of the "Femme Frenzy" event at the Inside/Out Toronto International Lesbian and Gay Film and Video Festival 2000, programmed, in fact, by Anna Camilleri and Chloë Brushwood Rose. I thank Anna and Chloë for taking the risks they did with all of the films and thank Inside/Out for making Saito's work available to me.

Chapter 6

CONCLUSION: ARCHIVE OF
POST-QUEER, INCOHERENT BODIES

It is exactly this lack of mastery, this productive failure to master the terms of identity, anxiety, and desire, that needs to be safeguarded and promoted in [...] risking identity's incoherence.

Calvin Thomas (2000: 32)

MY INCLUSION OF THE POLITICS OF FEMME AS A TRANS-GENDER IS clearly invested. I have been arguing here, with Thomas, that through a politic of incoherence that refuses hegemonic fictions of ontology and presence, trans subjectivities can do to whiteness and masculinity what femme redress does to femininity. That is, I assume that identity politics—where a singular privileged subject position is offered as the ground zero of a social movement—are ineffectual. If I am right, then what matters, as Foucault has clearly indicated, is a critical practice of resistance that refuses to allow power to articulate across and through coherent bodies, especially intersectional bodies, reducing them to one axis of identity only, regardless of what that axis might be. I am operating with a certain degree of political optimism here, admittedly. While the forces of conservatism are as potent and deadly as ever, I take a slight degree of comfort in watching for a politic of incoherence around me. There can be no better example of incoherence and dissolution— indeed, of transnationalism—than the 2004 American election. If a national identity, like those produced by engendering, racializations, capitalism, and so forth, are imaginary and operate best when rendered singular (what Anderson called an imagined fraternity), then a productive and distressing blow has been struck to that "American" imaginary (Anderson 1991: 15). This is not to say that the United States is any less fractured today than it was 50 years ago. But what is becoming increasingly fractured is an imaginary self-image, one for at least half of the U.S. (likely both halves albeit differently) that is becoming harder and harder to maintain. That is nowhere near the end point of our political imperatives. But if I am arguing that a queer practice is no longer as viable given the degree to which it fails to connote intersectionality, then what I offer instead is a practice of trans-incoherence. Such a practice troubles the singular fiction that is to accrue or cohere from the meeting point of intersections into a singular, ontological essence that we call self. My question has been and remains: What happens if we refuse that coherence and practise incoherence instead?

In this final chapter I document incoherent bodies through one film and analyses of photograph collections. The film is *Girl King* by Canadian filmmaker Ileana Pietrobruno. This film explores the post-queer incoherent body. The collections of photographs, *Body Alchemy: Transsexual Portraits* by Loren Cameron and *Sublime Mutations* by Del LaGrace Volcano, use the camera to document the intersexed (by-choice) genitals of this body and visualize a social and sometimes sexual affiliation between FtMs and both gay and straight masculinity. This affiliation, I argue, changes as the relation—indeed, process of becoming incoherently masculine—is put on display.

Ileana Pietrobruno's film *Girl King* is a delicious romp through No Man's Land that visualizes not only drag king cultures and fem(me)ininities but trans-bodies and desires as well. Made by a West Coast Canadian femme filmmaker, the pastiche's primary narrative tension spins around drag king pirates' quest for their Queen's Koilos, or source of all pleasures and harmony on her island. Queen is a powerful femme with a tremendously potent sexual appetite for boyz. The main boy character is named, of course, Butch, who must, if he fails to recover the treasured Koilos, give up his own stone butch virginity to the Queen as his punishment. If that were not incentive enough, Queen is holding Butch's love interest, the feisty femme Claudia, as hostage. Claudia decides not to wait for rescue and dons pirate garb to disguise herself as one of Butch's sexy shipmates sailing with Captain Candy in search of Queen's Koilos. In the end, Queen's Koilos is retrieved from the King who stole it; the King is himself, or so we discover through a series of turns, a drag king who actually gave birth to but eventually abandoned Butch, who was washed ashore as an infant in—what else?—a treasure chest. But this is where the choice of form is entirely telling. If we can assume a film has two audiences (one *to whom* it is directed; one *for whom* it is made), then *Girl King* is *directed at* female masculinity, trans masculinity, and drag kings, but *for* the pleasures of queer femme audience. That is to say, the film parodies and pokes fun at cultures of female and trans masculinities, and sometimes even queers gay masculinities (within each of which I am placing drag king cultures), but for the pleasures of a queer fem(me)inine gaze that undoes masculinity as it is being consumed. The primary cultures parodied, though, are drag king cultures and female masculinities. But like any parody, it has much to tell us about each.

Playing on several different narratives, including the boy's swashbuckling pirate adventure narrative, the quest motif, and a search-for-origins story, *Girl*

King situates the drag king himself as a central element in each of these narrative structures. And central to the work that drag king cultures do to and through masculinity are three crucial processes: recognition and misrecognition; identification but simultaneous dis-identification; and heteronormative desire but also a queering of each of these on the site of sexed bodies so that those bodies no longer register within a coherent dichotomous gay vs. straight economy. Let me take each of these in turn. First, recognition and misrecognition.

One of the key pleasures of drag king performances depends upon recognition of the contradiction at their source; that is, the recognition of a supposedly stable sexed body in distinction with the performance of masculinity written onto it. Part of this pleasure is irony, but another part of it are the pleasures of the incongruous spectacle itself. The performances of drag kings permanently rupture masculinity from the male body and reconfigure masculinity as a series of signifiers performable by anyone. We see this in *Girl King*, for instance, when Claudia cross-dresses as a boy or when Captain Candy teaches Butch how to *make the signifiers cohere more like a man*: prosthetics such as clothing, the appearance of facial hair, the swagger, facial expressions, and so on together accrue toward a masculine persona so that the fictional "truth" of the performance outweighs its authentic fictionality. The pleasures of drag kinging—indeed, of female masculinity writ large—lie somewhere between each pole. This is precisely what is so brilliantly ironic about *Girl King*, that is, its clever overlapping of form and content. Drag kings themselves perform a *pirated* version of masculinity, one plundered and, to pun on the term "pirate" itself, one "stolen" and used without authorization (*Oxford English Dictionary*). Pirating is such a powerful trope in postmodernity that theorists such as Jean Baudrillard have suggested that we've pirated so much, so thoroughly, that "originals" are no longer discernible or even knowable. We use the trope of pirating in so many places, why not use it as a trope of masculinity? Why cling so tenaciously to the idea of an essential (read: biological) masculinity if not only to maintain hegemonic power, albeit unconsciously? Pirating occurs as the narrative structure of *Girl King*, as well as in centralizing a drag king as the main character. But the formal visual structure itself is a performative, non-cohering pastiche of pirating; a multitude of images, motifs, and tropes are sutured together, with sutures in full sight, from many different sources, including lesbian scenes from heterosexual male porn, to recontextualize and, by implication, remake their now irreverent and tenacious meaning.

Similarly, the pleasures involved in performing masculinity lie in their ambivalent positionings between two further poles: identification and dis-identification. Numerous drag kings have detailed the degree to which they both identify with masculinity as a gender that hails them far more than conventional femininity does; at the same time, those hailings take place with a critical distance from conventionally defined male bodies. So, in the same way that boy cultures threaten incoherence as phallic failure, the difference between "boy" and "man" spins around the degree to which each resonates on the same frequency. Similarly, female-to-male trans-sexual men also productively *become* that incoherent phallic male body even as they simultaneously fully inhabit the fictional performance of that body (the way we see Butch, Captain Candy, and even Claudia do in *Girl King*). More than these examples, though, drag kings have as a goal the entire reconstruction of the illusion of embodiment, a prosthetic illusion that, as we have seen already, tells a more interesting story about the complexities of identification and dis-identification.

But so too do the images of the naked bodies and intersexed and FtM genitals photographed by Loren Cameron in his book, *Body Alchemy: Transsexual Portraits* (1996). Cameron's book was tremendously successful as it was one of the first to include a series of non-medicalized images of FtMs and their bodies. His book is structured in sections that document naked and clothed bodies, some before-and-after shots, and a series of self-portraits. Of course, the term "alchemy" in the title refers to the degree to which matter is transformed as a regular part of scientific practice; here, the transformations are, as the preface indicates, both prima material and ultima material, prime and ultimate, all witnessed by Cameron's camera. Cameron includes a series of self-portraits that show his sculptured white body making direct eye contact with the viewer. His body is facing the camera and as the eye travels across his body and follows his tattoos, what becomes evident is the incoherence of this flesh. His body signifies masculinity: chiselled face, developed musculature, absence of breasts, hair across his belly and upper thighs, and pubic area. But where one might expect to see a penis, one sees only pubic hair and shadow. This is incongruity writ large. Cameron's aesthetic is primarily realist documentary and his book remains extremely important for producing positive and non-medicalized trans portraits.

But Del LaGrace Volcano has done remarkable work in his photographs in *Sublime Mutations* (2000). Del has been using his camera to document and shape queer communities for at least two decades. His influential book, *Love Bites*, published under the name "Della Grace," was a series of photographs documenting lesbian bars and sex practices in the London lesbian and s/m communities in the 1980s. His work in that book made important interventions in the feminist sex wars by using the camera to freeze moments that spoke back to those debates. Del has also been instrumental in photographing drag kings across North America and Europe, and much of his work is featured in Gabriel Baur's drag king/FtM documentary called *Venus Boyz* (2003). But with *Sublime Mutations*, Del achieves a success and accomplishment with his camera unlike anyone before him. His remarkably queer, trans-formative, shape-shifting, and, true to form, sublime work with his camera details precisely the type of incoherence I call for in this book. As he puts it himself in the introduction:

> Bodies as sites of mutation, loss and longing have been my overriding and obsessional concerns for the past ten years. Sublime Mutations are the transformations that are produced by age, accident, illness, or design. The motto is: Mutate and survive or stagnate and perish. I've possessed and been possessed by a multitude of names, bodies and identities in my forty odd years. Change, mutation and migration are as natural to me as staying the same might be to you .... Mutations come in many forms ... I believe in crossing the line, not just once, but as many times as it takes to weave a web we can all walk on. (Volcano 2000: 5)

This is, as I indicated earlier, not crossing over just once, but bodies becoming so incoherent that they fail to register on our gender maps at all.

As Jay Prosser notes in his retrospective essay that introduces the photographs, "The Art of Ph/Autography: Del LaGrace Volcano," Del's aesthetic, like Cameron's, is documentary, establishing the "real" of masculinity and the "real" of trans-sexuality (Volcano 2000: 7). But where Prosser argues that Del's work is realist and documentary, I see an entirely different use of form, a far more stylized and hyper-real-ness that has as its effect the production of bodies outside of what is visible and considered "real" according to the laws of matter. That is, these images defamiliarize that "real" to make it unrecognizably *unreal* and incoherent as gendered embodiment. The images of FtM and intersexed genitals are incoherent given our tools for making sense of bodies. For instance, "Hermaphrodite Torso," performs this incoherence. Like Cameron's work, this photograph shows an intersexed body becoming itself, where a small penis seems to be emerging from labia. Chest surgical scars are not evident on the torso's chest, but between the nipples is calligraphy performatively marking the white body through what seems to be nonsense, no-sense. "Finger Food," Photo 5, one of a series of genital close-up photographs, cropped to foreground the central image, a richly textured

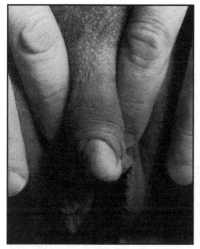

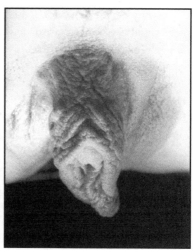

Photo 5: Finger Food. Del LaGrace
Volcano. Used with permission.

Photo 6: Stalagtite. Del LaGrace
Volcano. Used with permission.

small penis juxtaposed against four fingers that display it and against which that penis seems unreal in its size. Photo 6, "Stalactite" (literally, "a deposit of calcium carbonate formed like a large icicle hanging from the roof of a cave") again defies coherence. Its protruding and hanging shape is marked by tiny crevices and textured skin that articulate this image completely outside of the dichotomous male and female even as the head of a small penis/clitoris

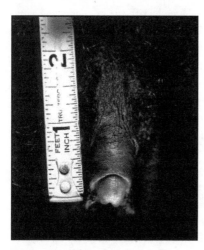

Photo 7: Transcock. Del LaGrace
Volcano. Used with permission.

is evident. Photo 7, "TransCock I," shows a Black penis measured ironically against a ruler of about 2.5 units long, although the ambiguity of the units of measurement—both feet and inches are visible—work against the connotations of the blackness of the skin. The connotations of the ruler as a supposed signifier of irrefutable Truth work against those signified by the blackness of the skin, producing an incoherent image of a non-phallic Black cock. This, of course, is significant in an economy where Black masculinity must strike hegemonic bargains for visibility, trading hyper-masculinity for credibility. These photographs are shocking in their revelatory nature, constructing *unreal* and incoherent bodies that cannot be easily placed within our sexed and gendered economies. In *Girl King*, Sailor's body is similarly incoherent and is another fascinating example of the type of corporeal destabilizations that I am drawing out in this book. One of the curious things about these destabilizations—that is, of masculinity from the essentialized male body—is that they are launched—and, by implication, can be restabilized—by desire. In many ways, the entire plot of *Girl King* is about desire and fantasy as the scene of those desires. Both the form and content stage fantasy for us; it takes place on a nowhere beach; its characters have names like "Butch" and "Sailor"; spliced into this swashbuckling, dress-up fantasy are queer appropriations from heterosexual "lesbian" porn mixed with scenes from gender play in lesbian porn; and the narrative crisis itself spins around whether or not Butch can retrieve the Queen's Koilos or else give up his stone, impenetrable virginity to (femme top) Queen as punishment for failing in his quest. Moreover, we see gay male desire equally parodied here as Butch and Claudia (passing as a boy) also flirt with phallic objects and eventually have sex dressed as two male shipmates, having both gay sex and lesbian sex at exactly the same moment. These are indeed incoherent scenes of queer(ed) desire.

But it isn't until the very butch Captain Candy hooks up with Sailor—who is, unbeknownst to Captain Candy, a male-to-female trans femme (in this context, someone who manipulates the illusion of possessing a female body)—that desire is post-queer; that is, literally off the gender maps as we currently know them. Captain Candy is drawn to a softness in Sailor, which he misrecognizes as biological femininity. Sailor also seems drawn to Captain Candy's gender and this mutuality makes their desires heterogendered—sexually attracted to gender difference—but not heteronormative. It isn't until after they've made initial sexual and physical contact with each other that Captain Candy eventually discovers what seems to be a "real" penis attached to Sailor's very feminine body. Of course, Candy disavows his attraction, but after some convincing, Candy resigns himself to the presence of a by now non-phallic penis, and asks, "Ok, how does this thing work?" (Photo 8a and 8b) The fascinating thing here, of course, is the queerness and post-queerness of this as a moment. Each partner is performing a gender opposite to that dictated by their respective body parts, but the presence of these supposedly self-evident sexed bodies does not in any way undo their genders. In fact, the illogical contradictions are quickly forgotten and almost virtually impossible to reconcile even in language. For instance, notice how the logic underwriting

Photo 8a, 8b: *Girl King*. Ileana Pietrobruno, dir. Captain Candy and Sailor. Used with permission.

the relation between bodies and genders is thoroughly undone in the question that begs to be asked about their off-screen genital sexual contact: If his (Captain Candy's) vagina has contact with her (Sailor's) penis, does that contact make this heterosexual sex? Clearly, the answer has to be no, not at all. The gendered meanings of each character trumps what the sex/gender system wants to inscribe onto their bodies. In fact, we could push this question even further: What kind of words and/or categories will we use to describe this sexual scene: Two men? Two women? A man and a woman? Which one is which? This is a scene of post-queer trans desire whose logic defies even a simple queering of their attraction for each other. It is a set of desires that defy logic, bodies, and the grammars of both the sex/gender system and even many of the attempts (well-meaning as they are) to deconstruct "gender" difference. We are left with a completely different relation between bodies and identities, which I referred to earlier as genders without genitals. These new trans-genders, I suggest, mark an important paradigm shift that we need to promote if the sons of the movement will succeed in remaking a masculinity incoherent enough to matter at all.

WORKS CITED

Allen, Theodore. 1994. *The Invention of the White Race. Volume 1: Racial Oppression and Social Control.* London: Verso.

Allison, Dorothy. 1994. *Skin: Talking about Sex, Class and Literature.* Ithaca: Firebrand Books.

Althusser, Louis. 1971. "Ideology and Ideological State Apparatuses." In *Lenin and Philosophy*, translated by Ben Brewster, 170–186. New York and London: Monthly Review Press.

Anderson, Benedict. 1991. *Imagined Communities: Reflections on the Origin and Spread of Nationalism.* London: Verso.

Anzaldúa, Gloria. 1991. "To(o) Queer the Writer: Loca, escrita y chicana." In *InVersions: Writings by Dykes, Queers and Lesbians*, edited by Betsy Warland, 249-263. Vancouver: Press Gang.

Bagnell, Kenneth. 1980. *The Little Immigrants: The Orphans Who Came to Canada.* Toronto: Macmillan of Canada.

Bakhtin, Mikhail. 1981. "Discourse in the Novel." In *The Dialogic Imagination*, Mikhail Bakhtin, 259–422. London: University of Texas Press.

_____. 1984. "Discourse in Dostoevsky." In *Problems of Dostoevsky's Poetics*. Manchester: Manchester University Press. 181-269.

_____. 1986. *Speech Genres and Other Late Essays.* London: University of Texas Press.

Bakhtin, Mikhail, and P. Medvedev. 1978. *The Formal Method in Literary Scholarship.* London: Johns Hopkins University Press.

Baldwin, James. 1985. *The Price of the Ticket: Collected Nonfiction 1948–1985.* New York: St. Martin's Press.

Baudrillard, Jean. 1995. *Simulacra and Simulation*, translated by Sheila Glaser. Ann Arbor: University of Michigan Press.

Bederman, Gail. 1995. *Manliness & Civilization: A Cultural History of Gender and Race in the United States, 1880–1917.* Chicago: University of Chicago Press.

Berger, John. 1972. *Ways of Seeing.* London: Penguin Books.

Bersani, Leo. 1995. "Loving Men." In *Constructing Masculinity*, edited by Maurice Berger, Brian Wallis, and Simon Watson, 116–123. New York and London: Routledge.

Bhabha, Homi. 1995. "Are You a Man or a Mouse?" In *Constructing Masculinity*, edited by Maurice Berger, Brian Wallis, and Simon Watson, 57–65. New York and London: Routledge.

Bly, Robert. 1990. *Iron John: A Book about Men.* Reading, MA: Addison-Wesley.

Brand, Dionne. 2002. *A Map to the Door of No Return.* Toronto: Coach House.

Butler, Judith. 1990. *Gender Trouble: Feminism and the Subversion of Identity.* New York and London: Routledge, Chapman & Hall, Inc.

_____. 1991. "Imitation and Gender Insubordination." In *Inside/Out: Lesbian Theories, Gay Theories,* edited by Diana Fuss, 1–31. New York: Routledge.

_____. 1993. *Bodies That Matter: On the Discursive Limits of "Sex."* New York and London: Routledge.

_____. 1997a. *Excitable Speech: A Politics of the Performative.* New York: Routledge.

_____. 1997b. "Melancholy Gender/Refused Identification." In *The Psychic Life of Power,* Judith Butler, 132–166. Stanford: Stanford University Press.

_____. 1998. "Afterword." In *Butch/Femme: Inside Lesbian Gender,* edited by Sally R. Munt, 225–230. London and Washington: Cassell.

_____. 2004. *Undoing Gender.* New York: Routledge.

Califia, Patrick. 1982. "A Personal View of the History of the Lesbian S/M Community and Movement in San Francisco." In *Coming to Power,* edited by SAMOIS, 243–281. Los Angeles: Alyson.

Cameron, Loren. 1996. *Body Alchemy: Transsexual Portraits.* Pittsburgh: Cleis Press.

Camilleri, Anna. 2004. *I Am a Red Dress: Incantations on a Grandmother, a Mother, and a Daughter.* Vancouver: Arsenal Pulp Press.

Camilleri, Anna, and Chloë Brushwood Rose. 2002. *Brazen Femme: Queering Femininity.* Vancouver: Arsenal Pulp Press.

Camilleri, Anna, Ivan E. Coyote, Zoë Eakle, and Lyndell Montgomery. 1998. "Taste This." *Boys Like Her: Transfictions.* Vancouver: Press Gang Publishers.

Case, Sue-Ellen. 1993. "Toward a Butch-Femme Aesthetic." In *The Lesbian and Gay Studies Reader,* edited by Henry Abelove, Michèle Aina Barale, and David M. Halperin, 294–306. New York: Routledge.

_____. 1995a. "Performing Lesbian in the Space of Technology: Part I." *Theatre Journal* 47: 1–18.

_____. 1995b. "Performing Lesbian in the Space of Technology: Part II." *Theatre Journal* 47: 329–343.

Cohan, Steve. 1997. *Masked Men: Masculinity and the Movies in the Fifties.* Bloomington and Indianapolis: Indiana University Press.

Colapinto, John. 2000. *As Nature Made Him: The Boy Who Was Raised as a Girl.* Toronto: HarperCollins Publishers.

Creet, Julia. 1991. "Daughters of the Movement: The Psychodynamics of Lesbian S/M Fantasy." *Differences: A Journal of Feminist Cultural Studies. Lesbian and Gay Sexualities* 3, no. 2: 135–159.

Crichlow, Wesley. 2004. *Buller Men and Batty Bwoys: Hidden Men in the Toronto and Halifax Black Communities.* Toronto: University of Toronto Press.

Cvetkovich, Ann. 2003. *An Archive of Feelings: Trauma, Sexuality and Lesbian Public Cultures.* Durham: Duke University Press.

Davy, Kate. 1994. "Fe/Male Impersonation: The Discourse of Camp." In *The Politics and Poetics of Camp,* edited by Moe Meyer, 130-148. London: Routledge.

———. 1995. "Outing Whiteness: A Feminist/Lesbian Project." *Theatre Journal* 47: 189–205.

De Beauvoir, Simone. 1953. *The Second Sex,* translated and edited by H.M. Parshley. New York : Vintage.

de Lauretis, Teresa. 1991. "Queer Theory: Lesbian and Gay Sexualities. An Introduction." *Differences: A Journal of Feminist Cultural Studies* 3, no. 2: iii–xviii.

———. 1993. "Sexual Indifference and Lesbian Representation." In *The Lesbian and Gay Studies Reader,* edited by Henry Abelove, Michèle Aina Barale, and David M. Halperin, 141–158. New York: Routledge.

———. 1997. "Technology of Gender." In *Technologies of Gender: Essays on Theory, Film and Fiction,* Teresa de Lauretis, 1–30. Bloomington: Indiana University Press.

Devor, Aaron. 1997. *FTM: Female-to-Male Transsexuals in Society.* Bloomington: Indiana University Press.

Doan, Laura. 1994. "Jeanette Winterson's Sexing the Postmodern." In *The Lesbian Postmodern,* edited by Laura Doan, 137–155. New York: Columbia University Press.

Dolan, Jill. 1988. "The Discourse of Feminisms: The Spectator and Representation." In *The Feminist Spectator as Critic,* edited by Jill Dolan, 1–18. Ann Arbor: UMI Research Press.

———. 1990. "'Lesbian' Subjectivity in Realism: Dragging at the Margins of Structure and Ideology." In *Performing Feminisms: Feminist Critical Theory and Theatre,* edited by Sue-Ellen Case, 40–53. Baltimore: The John Hopkins University Press.

———. 1993. "Geographies of Learning: Theatre Studies, Performance, and the 'Performative.'" *Theatre Journal* 45: 417–441.

Dollimore, Jonathan. 1991. *Sexual Dissidence: Augustine to Wilde, Freud to Foucault.* Oxford: Clarendon Press.

Dotson, Edisol Wayne. 1999. *Behold the Man: The Hype and Selling of Male Beauty in Media and Culture.* New York: Harrington Park Press.

DuBois, W. E. B. 1990 (1903). *The Souls of Black Folk.* New York: Random House.

Duggan, Lisa, and Kathleen McHugh. 1996. "A Fem(me)inist Manifesto." *Women & Performance: A Journal of Feminist Theory* 8, no. 2: 107–110.

Dyer, Richard. 1988. "White." *Screen* 29, no. 4: 44–64.

———. 1997. *White.* London and New York: Routledge.

Elliott, Patricia. 1998. "Some Critical Reflections on the Transgender Theory of Kate Bornstein." *Atlantis* 23.1: 14–21.

Evans, Caroline, and Lorraine Gamman. 1995. "The Gaze Revisited, or Reviewing Queer Viewing." In *A Queer Romance: Lesbians, Gay Men and Popular Culture,* edited by Paul Burston and Colin Richardson, 13–56. London: Routledge.

Eugenides, Jeffrey. 2002. *Middlesex*. Toronto: Random House.

Fausto-Sterling, Anne. 2000. *Sexing the Body: Gender Politics and the Construction of Sexuality*. New York: Basic Books.

Feinberg, Leslie. 1991. *Stone Butch Blues*. Ithaca, NY: Firebrand.

Findlay, Heather. 2003. "Editorial." *Girlfriends: Lesbian Culture, Politics, and Entertainment*. March, 2003.

Foucault, Michel. 1977. *Language, Counter-memory, Practice: Selected Essays and Interviews by Michel Foucault*, edited by Donald F. Bouchard, 139–164. Ithaca: Cornell University Press.

_____. 1982. *The History of Sexuality. Volume 1: An Introduction*, translated by Robert Hurley. New York: Random House.

_____. 1979. *Discipline and Punish: The Birth of the Prison*, translated by Alan Sheridan. New York: Vintage.

Frankenberg, Ruth. 1993. *White Women, Race Matters: The Social Construction of Whiteness*. Minneapolis: University of Minnesota Press.

Fuss, Diana. 1995. *Identification Papers*. New York: Routledge.

Gardiner, Judith Kegan, ed. 2002. *Masculinity Studies and Feminist Theory: New Directions*. New York: Columbia University Press.

Gledhill, Christine, ed. 1991. *Stardom: Industry of Desire*. New York: Routledge.

Goldman, Ruth. 1996. "Who Is That *Queer* Queer? Exploring Norms around Sexuality, Race, and Class in Queer Theory." In *Queer Studies: A Lesbian, Gay, Bisexual and Transgender Anthology*, edited by Brett Beemyn and Mickey Eliason, 169–182. New York: New York University Press.

Griggers, Camilla. 1997. *Becoming-Woman*. Minneapolis: University of Minnesota Press.

Halberstam, Judith. 1994. "F2M: The Making of Female Masculinity." In *The Lesbian Postmodern*, edited by Laura Doan, 210–228. New York: Columbia University Press.

_____. 1998a. *Female Masculinity*. Durham and London: Duke University Press.

_____, and C. Jacob Hale. 1998b. "Transgender Butch: Butch/FTM Border Wars and the Masculine Continuum." *GLQ: A Journal of Lesbian and Gay Studies. The Transgender Issue* 4, no. 2: 287–310.

Hall, Stuart. 1996. "For Allon White: Metaphors of Transformation." In *Stuart Hall: Critical Dialogues in Cultural Studies*, edited by David Morley and Kuan-Hsing Chen, 287–305. London and New York: Routledge.

Hill, Darryl B. 2002. "Review of Female Masculinity." *Journal of Men's Studies* 10, no. 2: 237–239.

Pope Jr., Harrison G., Katharine A. Phillips, and Roberto Olivardia. 2000. *The Adonis Complex*. New York: Simon & Schuster.

Hart, Lynda. 1993. "Identity and Seduction: Lesbians in the Mainstream." In *Acting Out: Feminist Performances*, edited by Lynda Hart and Peggy Phelan, 119–137. Ann Arbor: The University of Michigan Press.

———. 1994. *Fatal Women: Lesbian Sexuality and the Mark of Aggression*. Princeton: Princeton University Press.

———. 1998. *Between the Body and the Flesh: Performing Sadomasochism*. New York: Columbia University Press.

Hemmings, Clare. 1999. "Out of Sight, Out of Mind? Theorizing Femme Narrative." *Sexualities* 2, no. 4: 387–396.

Henry, Astrid. 2004. *Not My Mother's Sister: Generational Conflict and Third Wave Feminism*. Indianapolis: Indiana University Press.

Henson, Leslie J. 1997. "Articulate Silence(s): Femme Subjectivity and Class Relations in *The Well of Loneliness*." In *Femme: Feminists Lesbians & Bad Girls*, edited by Laura Harris and Elizabeth Crocker, 61–67. New York and London: Routledge.

hooks, bell. 1992. "The Oppositional Gaze." In *Black Looks: Race and Representation*, ed. bell hooks, 115–131. Toronto: Between the Lines.

———. 2000. *Where We Stand: Class Matters*. New York and London: Routledge.

———. 2004. *We Real Cool: Black Men and Masculinity*. New York: Routledge.

Jardine, Alice and Paul Smith, eds. 1987. *Men in Feminism*. New York: Metheun.

Johnson, Barbara. 1987. *A World of Difference*. Baltimore and London: The Johns Hopkins University Press.

Jones, Jordy. 2004. "Gender without Genitals: Hedwig's Six Inches." 6th International Congress on Sex and Gender Diversity: Reflecting Genders, Manchester Metropolitan University.

Kaplan, E. Ann. 1997. *Looking for the Other: Feminism, Film, and the Imperial Gaze*. New York and London: Routledge.

Kessler, Suzanne S. and Woody McKenna. 1978. *Gender: An Ethnomethodological Approach*. Chicago: University of Chicago Press.

Lapovsky Kennedy, Elizabeth and Madeline Davis. 1993. *Boots of Leather, Slippers of Gold: The History of a Lesbian Community*. New York: Penguin.

Ledger, Brent. 1998. "Getting to Know Dick: Transsexuals Are Guardians of Gender Status Quo." *Xtra!* 357: 37.

MacDonald, Eleanor. 1998. "Critical Identities: Rethinking Feminism through Transgender Politics." *Atlantis* 23, no.1 (Fall/Winter): 3–12.

Martin, Biddy. 1996. *Femininity Played Straight: The Significance of Being Lesbian*. New York and London: Routledge.

Martin, Del, and Phyllis Lyon. 1972. *Lesbian/Woman*. San Francisco: Glide Publications.

Martindale, Kathleen. 1996. *The Making of an Un/popular Culture: From Lesbian Feminism to Lesbian Postmodernism*. New York: SUNY Press.

Mercer, Kobena. 1994, *Welcome to the Jungle: New Positions in Black Cultural Studies*. New York: Routledge.

Minkowitz, Donna. 1994. "Love Hurts." *Village Voice* (April 19): 24–30.

Modleski, Tania. 1991. *Feminism without Women: Culture and Criticism in a Postfeminist Age*. London: Routledge.

Morrison, Toni. 1992. *Playing in the Dark: Whiteness and the Literary Imagination*. Cambridge, MA: Harvard.

Mulvey, Laura. 1989. "Visual Pleasure and Narrative Cinema." In *Visual and Other Pleasures*, Laura Mulvey, 14–26. Bloomington and Indianapolis: Indiana University Press.

Muñoz, José Esteban. 1999. *Disidentifications: Queers of Colour and the Performance of Politics*. Minneapolis: University of Minnesota Press.

Munt, Sally, ed. 1998a. *Butch/Femme: Inside Lesbian Gender*. London: Cassell.

_____. 1998b. *Heroic Desire: Lesbian Identity and Cultural Space*. New York: New York University Press.

Namaste, Vivane. 2005. *Sex Change, Social Change: Reflections on Identity, Institutions, and Imperialism*. Toronto: Women's Press.

Nestle, Joan. 1987. *A Restricted Country*. Los Angeles: Alyson.

_____. 1992. *The Persistent Desire: A Femme-Butch Reader*. Los Angeles: Alyson.

Newman, Lesléa. 1995. *The Femme Mystique*. Los Angeles: Alyson.

Newitz, Annalee. 1997. "White Savagery and Humiliation, or a New Racial Consciousness in the Media." In *White Trash: Race and Class in America*, edited by Matt Wray and Annalee Newitz, 131–154. New York: Routledge.

Newton, Esther. 1989. "The Mythic Mannish Lesbian: Radclyffe Hall and the New Woman." In *Hidden from History: Reclaiming the Gay and Lesbian Past*, eds. Martin Duberman, Martha Vicinus, and George Chauncey, Jr., 281–293. New York: Penguin Books.

Nietzsche, Friedrich. 1887. *The Gay Science*, trans. Walter Kauffman (1968). New York: Random House. In *Basic Writings of Friedrich Nietzsche*.

Nixon vs. Vancouver Rape Relief Society. 2002. British Columbia Human Rights Tribunal.

Noble, Jean Bobby. 2004. *Masculinities without Men?* Vancouver: University of British Columbia Press.

Ouellete, Marc. 2005. "'See Me, Touch Me, Feel Me': (Im)Proving the Bodily Sense of Masculinity." Available online at www.reconstruction.ws/024/ouellete.htm.

Parker, Andrew, and Eve Kosofsky Sedgwick, eds. 1995. *Performativity and Performance*. New York: Routledge.

Phelan, Peggy. 1993a. "Reciting the Citation of Others; or, a Second Introduction." In *Acting Out: Feminist Performances*, edited by Lynda Hart and Peggy Phelan, 13–31. Ann Arbor: The University of Michigan Press.

_____. 1993b. "White Men and Pregnancy: Discovering the Body to Be Rescued." In *Acting Out: Feminist Performances*, edited by Lynda Hart and Peggy Phelan, 383-401. Ann Arbor: The University of Michigan Press.

_____. 1993c. *Unmarked: The Politics of Performance*. New York: Routledge.

Pollack, William. 1998. *Real Boys: Rescuing Our Sons from the Myths of Boyhood*. New York: Henry Holt and Company.

Pope, Harrison G., Katharine A. Phillips, and Roberto Olivardia. 2000. *The Adonis Complex*. New York: Simon and Schuster.

Probyn, Elspeth. 1995. "Lesbians in Space: Gender, Sex and the Structure of Missing." *Gender, Place and Culture* 2, no. 1: 77–84.

Prosser, Jay. 1997. "Transgender." In *Lesbian and Gay Studies: A Critical Introduction*, edited by Andy Medhurst and Sally R. Munt, 309–326. London and Washington: Cassell.

_____. 1998. *Second Skins: The Body Narratives of Transsexuality*. New York: Columbia University Press.

Riley, Denise. 1988. *"Am I That Name?": Feminism and the Category of "Women" in History*. Houndmills: Macmillan Press.

Robertson, Pamela. 1999. "What Makes the Feminist Camp?" In *Camp: Queer Aesthetics and the Performing Subject: A Reader*, edtied by Fabio Cleto, 266–282. Michigan: University of Michigan Press.

Roediger, David. 1999. *The Wages of Whiteness: Race and the Making of the American Working Class*. London: Verso.

_____. 1994. *Towards the Abolition of Whiteness: Essays on Race, Politics, and Working Class History*. London: Verson.

Rubin, Gayle. 1975. "The Traffic in Women: Notes on the 'Political Economy' of Sex." In *Toward an Anthropology of Women*, edited by Rayna R. Reiter, 157–210. New York: Monthly Review.

_____. 1984. "Thinking Sex: Notes for a Radical Theory of the Politics of Sexuality." *Pleasure and Danger: Exploring Female Sexuality*, edited by Carole Vance, 267–319. Boston: Routledge.

_____. 1992. "Of Catamites and Kings: Reflections on Butch, Gender, and Boundaries." In *The Persistent Desire: A Femme-Butch Reader*, edited by Joan Nestle, 466–482. Boston: Alyson Publications.

_____. 1994. "Sexual Traffic." *Differences: A Journal of Feminist Cultural Studies. More Gender Trouble: Feminism Meets Queer Theory* 6, no. 2–3: 62–99.

Schacht, Steven P. and Doris Ewing, eds. 1998. *Feminism and Men: Reconstructing Gender Relations*. New York: New York University Press.

Sedgwick, Eve Kosofsky. 1985. *Between Men: English Literature and Male Homosocial Desire*. New York: Columbia University Press.

———. 1990. *Epistemology of the Closet*. Berkeley and Los Angeles: University of California Press.

———. 1992. "Nationalisms and Sexualities in the Age of Wilde." In *Nationalisms and Sexualities*, edited by Andrew Parker, Mary Russo, Doris Sommer, and Patricia Yaeger, 235–245. New York: Routledge.

———. 1993. "Queer Performativity: Henry James's *The Art of the Novel*." *GLQ: A Journal of Lesbian and Gay Studies* 1, no. 1: 1–16.

———. 1995. "Gosh, Boy George, You Must Be Awfully Secure in Your Masculinity!" In *Constructing Masculinity*, edited by Maurice Berger, Brian Wallis, and Simon Watson, 11–20. New York and London: Routledge.

Simpson, Mark. 1994. *Male Impersonators: Men Performing Masculinity*. New York: Routledge.

Stoltenberg, John. 1990. *Refusing to Be a Man*. New York: Penguin Books.

Striker, Susan. 1998. "The Transgender Issue: An Introduction." *GLQ: A Journal of Lesbian and Gay Studies* 4, no. 2: 145–158.

Thomas, Calvin. 1996. *Male Matters: Masculinity, Anxiety, and the Male Body on the Line*. Urbana and Chicago: University of Illinois Press.

———. 2000. "Straight with a Twist." In *Straight with a Twist: Queer Theory and the Subject of Heterosexuality*, edited by Calvin Thomas, 11–44. Urbana and Chicago: University of Illinois Press.

Vance, Carole S. ed. 1983. "More Danger, More Pleasure: A Decade after the Barnard Sexuality Conference." In *Pleasure and Danger*, ed. Carole S. Vance, xvi–xxxix. London: Pandora.

Volcano, Del LaGrace. 2000. *Sublime Mutations*. Tübingen: Konkursbuch Verlag Claudia Gehrke.

Wagner, Gillian. 1997. *Children of the Empire*. London: Weidenfeld and Nicolson.

Walcott, Rinaldo. 1997. *Black Like Who? Writing. Black. Canada.* Toronto: Insomniac Press.

Wallace, Robert. 1996. "Performance Anxiety: 'Identity,' 'Community,' and Tim Miller's *My Queer Body*." *Modern Drama* 39: 97–116.

Film and Video

8 Mile. (video recording) Produced by Brian Grazer, Curtis Kitson, and Jimmy Iovine; directed by Curtis Hanson; written by Scott Silver. Imagine Entertainment, 2003.

Boys Don't Cry. (video recording) Directed by Kimberly Peirce. Twentieth-Century Fox Home Entertainment, 1999.

Fight Club. (video recording) ; Screenplay by Jim Uhls; produced by Art Linson, Cean Chaffin, and Ross Grayson Bell; directed by David Fincher. Fox 2000 Pictures and Regency Enterprises present a Linson Films production.